Devin Miller

BIBLE BASICS

BIBLE BASICS

**MASTERING
THE CONTENT
OF THE BIBLE**

Duncan S. Ferguson

WESTMINSTER JOHN KNOX PRESS
Louisville, Kentucky

To
faithful and dedicated preachers, biblical scholars,
and teachers from varied traditions and points of view
who have enriched my life by giving me
the Bible.

© 1995 Duncan S. Ferguson

All rights reserved. No part of this book may be reproduced or transmitted in any form or by any means, electronic or mechanical, including photocopying, recording, or by any information storage or retrieval system, without permission in writing from the publisher. For information, address Westminster John Knox Press, 100 Witherspoon Street, Louisville, Kentucky 40202-1396.

Book design by Publishers' WorkGroup
Cover design by Kevin Darst

First edition

Published by Westminster John Knox Press
Louisville, Kentucky

This book is printed on acid-free paper that meets the American National Standards Institute Z39.48 standard. ♾

PRINTED IN THE UNITED STATES OF AMERICA

95 96 97 98 99 00 01 02 03 04 — 10 9 8 7 6 5 4 3 2 1

Library of Congress Cataloging-in-Publication Data

Ferguson, Duncan S. (Duncan Sheldon), 1937–.
    Bible basics : mastering the content of the Bible / Duncan S. Ferguson. — 1st ed.
        p.   cm.
    Includes bibliographical references and index.
    ISBN 0-664-25570-1 (alk. paper)
    1. Bible—Handbooks, manuals, etc. I. Title.
BS417.F47 1995
220.6′ 1—dc20   95-11873

Contents

Preface   vi

Acknowledgments   vii

Part One. Finding Our Way into the Bible

1. Making the Bible Our Book   3
2. Orientation to Bible Study   9

Part Two. The Hebrew Bible (The Old Testament)

3. The Pentateuch   19
4. The Prophets   26
5. The Writings   44

Part Three. The New Testament

6. The Gospels   57
7. The Early Christian Community:
   Acts and the Pauline Epistles   66
8. The General Epistles and Revelation   82

Appendix A. Sample Tests   92

Appendix B. Maps and Charts   148

Appendix C. Suggested Reading List   159

Notes   163

Preface

The initial motivation for writing this book grew out of the observation that many theological seminary students and graduates have some anxiety about passing the Bible content segment in their ordination examinations. There are many Bible commentaries, Bible dictionaries, and Bible introductions, all of which are helpful, but few of these volumes aim specifically at assisting students with the examinations.

A second motivation is that many dedicated Christian people lack basic information about the Bible. Not having had extensive exposure to the content of the Bible in Sunday school classes, these Christians find the Bible a bit formidable and inaccessible. This volume is designed to help Christians augment their knowledge of the Bible and embrace it as a primary resource for spiritual nurture and guidance.

The focus is on the "facts," inasmuch as the facts are available to us. As with all reading of history, scholars debate what really happened. I have tried to steer away from the complex tasks of interpretation and ascribing meaning, although it is impossible to remain entirely free from presuppositions. The starting point in this project is that the Bible is "the rule of faith and practice" for the church.

The book has four major sections. The first provides some guidelines for getting the most from the book. Seminary students and graduates may want to move directly to the second section, which invites the reader into the fascinating world of the Hebrew Bible (the Old Testament). That world is quite different from our own, and the names and places of the Old Testament setting, the ancient Middle East, are not a part of our everyday conversation and reading. The third section deals with the New Testament and its more familiar characters and stories. The final section consists of appendixes, which provide sample quizzes that test how well the reader has mastered the factual content of the Bible, helpful maps and charts, and a list of additional resources for studying the Bible.

Acknowledgments

A book project always involves several people. I want to thank the staff of Westminster John Knox Press, and especially Jon Berquist, whose editorial advice helped bring the project to completion. In addition, I want to thank my colleagues in the Presbyterian Center for their help, patience, and grace in allowing me to spend the required preparation time.

The scripture quotations are from the New Revised Standard Version of the Bible, copyright © 1989, by the Division of Christian Education of the National Council of the Churches of Christ in the United States of America, and are used by permission.

Of the many works I consulted, four volumes in particular helped me in this effort to make the Bible accessible to all readers. They are: *Harper's Bible Dictionary,* by Paul J. Achtemeier, general editor, Harper & Row, San Francisco, 1985; *Understanding the Bible,* by Stephen L. Harris, 3d ed., Mayfield Publishing Co., Mountain View, Calif., 1992; *An Introduction to the Bible: A Journey into Three Worlds,* by Christian E. Hauer and William A. Young, 3d ed., Prentice-Hall, Englewood Cliffs, N.J., 1994; and *Harper's Bible Commentary,* by James L. Mays, general editor, Harper & Row, San Francisco, 1988.

As always, I am grateful to my family, Dorothy and Brian, who gave me the space and support necessary for this endeavor.

PART ONE

FINDING OUR WAY INTO THE BIBLE

1

Making the Bible
Our Book

Biblical Literacy

For most people in the United States, and indeed, in nearly all countries of the world, the Bible is an unused and unfamiliar book. Even those who are faithful in their attendance in church and synagogue are not knowledgeable about the contents of the Bible. The curious and sad irony here is that many devout religious people who claim the Bible as the primary sourcebook for their faith do not have a good grasp of its contents. And others, if only for educational reasons, need a basic understanding of the Bible to appreciate their cultural traditions.[1]

Religious institutions have certainly tried to meet the problem of biblical illiteracy. Synagogue and church schools offer Bible courses and classes for all ages, as well as religious resources. The KERYGMA[2] series has been used widely in Protestant denominations as a supplement to regularly scheduled Bible classes. But people are busy and distracted, and they have little time or interest in engaging in Bible study. The secular character of our culture, which influences us all, does not incline us to Bible study, which is usually viewed as a religious endeavor.

Yet we need the spiritual nurture, guidance, and comfort that come from gaining knowledge, insight, and perspective from the sacred literature of our heritage. The Bible is an extraordinary resource for all—both for those who stand within faith and those who have no religious commitments. It is a book that nurtures religious faith, gives comfort to the troubled, provides ethical guidance to the confused, and offers direction for the future to those who seek to find their way. It contains uncommon wisdom.

The trick is to make the Bible our book. For most of us, it is a question of motivation, time, and resources. Is it worth our energy to gain some mastery of the Bible? It does require some energy, for the Bible is a complex book. Is it of high enough priority that we will give serious Bible study an important place in our busy lives? It probably will require that we place

Bible study ahead of some other activity. Are there resources to help us gain access to a book from which we are separated by language, history, and culture? Yes, there are resources, although it may take some effort to obtain them. I hope that motivation will be present, that time will be found, and that this volume and the many others available will help give the treasure of the Bible to all who want to discover its riches.

Making the Most of This Book

This book is designed for the ordination candidate who seeks to pass the Bible content part of the ordination examination *and* for the busy person who wants a factual grasp of the Bible. It is a resource intended to be placed alongside the Bible and used as a helpful tool in the reading of the Bible. Some might argue that the text of the Bible is all one needs and that reference books and commentaries are simply a distraction. That can be true for some types of reading. Devotional reading, perhaps from the Psalms, might best be done without the assistance of resource materials. To read with openness, allowing the insight and force of the text to speak for itself, can be of great value. But if one reads for a factual understanding of the Bible, it is wise to have the assistance of good scholarship.

I have organized this book very simply to accommodate people on the run. The beginning provides a basic orientation to the study of the Bible. Included in this orientation is an overview of the Bible, which seeks to capture the big picture. The parts make better sense in light of the whole. One might view this attempt to state a unifying theme of the Bible (fraught with the danger of oversimplification and distortion as it is) as a large circle containing increasingly smaller circles within it. As a smaller circle, each section or genre in the Bible, then, is briefly described and placed in the context of the larger circle. (See fig. 1.) For example, the first five books of the Hebrew Bible, called the Pentateuch, are a natural grouping and have a particular place in the Bible and in religious communities that claim the Bible as their primary sourcebook for guidance on belief and practice.

The introduction to each category of books is followed by a description of each book in the grouping, the smallest circle. The description lists five easily remembered, straightforward categories introduced by one-word questions: Who? What? Where? When? and Why? The Who? section introduces the author, the intended readers, and the main chareacters in the story. The What? section tells the story and states the essential content of the book. The Where? and When? sections give basic geographical and historical information. The Why? section describes the author's

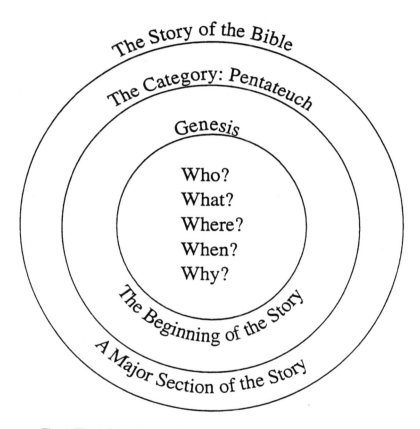

Fig. 1. The relationship of Genesis and the Pentateuch to the Bible

intention and the main themes of the book. The book of Genesis is used here to illustrate this approach.

WHO? The book of Genesis has many characters, but some of the most notable are Adam and Eve, Abraham and Sarah, Moses and Miriam.

WHAT? God creates; Abraham and Sarah (Abram and Sarai) go west and settle; Moses leads the exodus.

WHERE? The ancient Middle and Near East, with specific locations highlighted.

WHEN? From primeval history to about 1300 B.C.E., with key dates listed.

WHY? To tell the story of beginnings and foundations with major themes such as creation, covenant, and law.

In addition to basic information, charts and maps are provided to enable the reader to place the information in relationship to the larger story and themes of the Bible. For example, where does Paul travel on his missionary journeys? What routes does he take? What cities does he visit? Specific scholarly problems surrounding the "facts" are also discussed. It is not easy, for example, to state the precise date of the exodus from Egypt. Our first chart, a listing of the books of the Bible, will give us our bearings.

The Old Testament

Genesis	2 Chronicles	Daniel
Exodus	Ezra	Hosea
Leviticus	Nehemiah	Joel
Numbers	Esther	Amos
Deuteronomy	Job	Obadiah
Joshua	Psalms	Jonah
Judges	Proverbs	Micah
Ruth	Ecclesiastes	Nahum
1 Samuel	Song of Solomon	Habakkuk
2 Samuel	Isaiah	Zephaniah
1 Kings	Jeremiah	Haggai
2 Kings	Lamentations	Zechariah
1 Chronicles	Ezekiel	Malachi

The New Testament

Matthew	Ephesians	Hebrews
Mark	Philippians	James
Luke	Colossians	1 Peter

John	1 Thessalonians	2 Peter
Acts of the Apostles	2 Thessalonians	1 John
Romans	1 Timothy	2 John
1 Corinthians	2 Timothy	3 John
2 Corinthians	Titus	Jude
Galatians	Philemon	Revelation

Over the years it has been extremely helpful to me to be very familiar with the order of the books of the Bible. Although most Bibles have a table of contents that lists page numbers, it is still an advantage to have the sequence of the books well in mind so as to locate Bible passages quickly. To commit the lists to memory is not difficult and will serve the Bible user well.

Throughout this book, and in many other resource books, abbreviations are commonly used for the books of the Bible. As a general rule, the following abbreviations will be used here:

Old Testament

Gen	Genesis	2 Chr	2 Chronicles	Dan	Daniel
Ex	Exodus	Ezra	Ezra	Hos	Hosea
Lev	Leviticus	Neh	Nehemiah	Joel	Joel
Num	Numbers	Esth	Esther	Am	Amos
Deut	Deuteronomy	Job	Job	Ob	Obadiah
Josh	Joshua	Ps	Psalms	Jon	Jonah
Judg	Judges	Prov	Proverbs	Mic	Micah
Ruth	Ruth	Eccl	Ecclesiastes	Nah	Nahum
1 Sam	1 Samuel	Song	Song of Solomon	Hab	Habakkuk
2 Sam	2 Samuel	Isa	Isaiah	Zeph	Zephaniah
1 Kings	1 Kings	Jer	Jeremiah	Hag	Haggai
2 Kings	2 Kings	Lam	Lamentations	Zech	Zechariah
1 Chr	1 Chronicles	Ezek	Ezekiel	Mal	Malachi

New Testament

Mt	Matthew	Eph	Ephesians	Heb	Hebrews
Mk	Mark	Phil	Philippians	Jas	James
Lk	Luke	Col	Colossians	1 Pet	1 Peter
Jn	John	1 Thess	1 Thessalonians	2 Pet	2 Peter
Acts	Acts of the Apostles	2 Thess	2 Thessalonians	1 Jn	1 John
		1 Tim	1 Timothy	2 Jn	2 John
Rom	Romans	2 Tim	2 Timothy	3 Jn	3 John
1 Cor	1 Corinthians	Titus	Titus	Jude	Jude
2 Cor	2 Corinthians	Philem	Philemon	Rev	Revelation
Gal	Galatians				

Additional charts and maps, verbatim quizzes from ordination examinations, and a list of resources for those who want to make the Bible their own book are located in appendixes at the end of this book.

The first question when studying the Bible is which version to use. Seminary students and graduates understand the differences among the translations and thus may prefer one over the other. Because there are so many excellent translations of the Bible, however, it is not always easy to choose, especially for the uninitiated. Some English versions of the Bible are quite literal translations, ones in which an effort has been made to reproduce a very close rendering of the Hebrew (Old Testament) and Greek (New Testament) in English. An example of a very literal translation is the *New International Version.* Still other English versions put greater emphasis on capturing the meaning of a sentence or paragraph and rendering the thought in a well-constructed English sentence. Such versions are occasionally called paraphrases; a good example is J. B. Phillips's *The New Testament in Modern English,* or *The Living Bible.*

There are also differences in the English-language phrasing; some translations use more formal wording and attempt to preserve the elegance and beauty of the *King James Version.* The *New Revised Standard Version* (NRSV) is a good example of this kind of translation, and most quotations and references in this book are taken from the NRSV. Still others select phrasing that reflects our culture's use of English. In these versions contemporary idioms are not uncommon. *The Living Bible* is also a good example of a translation that uses informal, contemporary English.

In addition to a modern translation of the Bible, you will need a few basic reference books. For starters, I would recommend a Bible dictionary, a one-volume commentary, and a Bible atlas. Again, many are available, and a list of current reference works is included in Appendix C.

The goal is to make the Bible your book, to pick it up and read it with confidence, to build a solid historical and factual foundation, and to gain some competence in ascribing meaning to the sections you read. An important dimension in acquiring this level of mastery is to have some introductory information about the Bible and how best to read and study it. In addition, a good understanding of the story of the Bible and its foundational themes shows the relation of the parts to the whole. Chapter 2 provides this basic orientation to Bible study.

2

Orientation to Bible Study

On Reading the Story of the Bible

Part of the Bible's remarkable beauty and power is that it tells a story or many stories that together make a much longer story. And we love stories. They have a way of capturing our attention and imagination, especially if they are good stories, full of drama, emotion, and insight. As we hear a good story, we have several reactions. For example, we might note the literary quality of the story. The story was well crafted and written with polish and subtlety. Or we might remark that the story took us into another historical era, a fascinating world unlike our own. Often we say that the story had power "for me"; that is, the subjects and emotional sensitivity spoke to my experience.

The Bible is a piece of literature, and when we read it, we find ourselves in a *literary world,* or the world of the Bible text itself. This world is created for us by the stories and the many other types of literature in the Bible. As we study the Bible from a literary perspective, we generally set aside questions of history and tradition, which are "outside" the text. Our focus is rather on how the language of the Bible creates a world of meaning. Biblical scholars, keenly aware of the literary character of the Bible, have developed quite sophisticated literary approaches to the study of the Bible.[1]

The events described in the Bible, and the writing of the Bible, occurred in a larger historical context. The Bible makes reference to the surrounding world, a world of custom and conflict, culture and politics, economics and religious and philosophical points of view. The Bible emerges from a *historical world.* The historical setting of the Bible is the ancient Near East, with many of the dramas unfolding in ancient Israel. The first historical references in it go back to approximately 2000 B.C.E. and culminate at about 150 C.E.[2] Our reading of the Bible is greatly enhanced by a study of the history in which the Bible is enmeshed.

The Bible has an impact on us as we read it. We bring to our reading a range of assumptions, our life experiences, and our current situation, and we interpret the Bible through these lenses. The Bible in turn has a way of inviting reflection about our lives and polishing our lenses. The Bible has relevance in our *contemporary world*. We most often read the Bible to find guidance, comfort, and nurture for our lives. We are interested in what the Bible may have meant to its original readers, but even more important is what it means to each of us now and those about whom we care.

There are, then, at least three perspectives on the reading of the Bible: the literary, the historical, and the contemporary.[3] Each has its place as we attempt to understand the story of the Bible.

The Nature of the Bible

Many biblical scholars refer to the unity of the Bible and the interconnectedness of the Testaments.[4] They mean that some common thread or unifying theme gives the story of the Bible coherence and integrity. But this coherence is not easy to spot, and what is more obvious is the great diversity of literature the Bible contains. One might well ask on what grounds is it possible to maintain that the Bible has some unifying theme or core. Does the scholar find the unity inherent in the text of the Bible, or is the unity imposed from the presuppositions of the reader?

Several scholars have based the claim for unity on theological arguments. Karl Barth, a noted twentieth-century Christian theologian, maintained that Jesus Christ provides the unifying theme of the Bible. The Bible is essentially about God's self-disclosure, the Old Testament being the gradual unfolding of this disclosure and the New Testament being the full self-revelation of God in Jesus Christ. A similar argument is made for the unity of the Bible with the construct of promise and fulfillment. The underlying assumption in this view is that God has a purpose for all of history. The promise of God's design is contained in the Old Testament, and the coming of Christ in the New Testament is the fulfillment of the divine purpose. Often, the notion of covenant is placed at the center of the promise and fulfillment construct, providing the unifying center to the Bible. In both the Abrahamic and Mosaic covenants, God promises by covenant to bless, and in Jesus Christ, the covenant promise is realized. Still another variation of the theological argument is the contention that both Testaments share common themes. The presence of concepts about God and the human situation give the variety of writings some unity.

Underlying many of these theological arguments is the assumption of progressive revelation (a concept more widely accepted and used in an earlier generation). In this view, God gradually unfolds the divine will and purpose for human history across the centuries. The person, mission, and message of Jesus represent the high point of this progressive revelation, with the culmination promised in the prophetic passages. A related concept, that of canon (meaning rule or standard), has been employed for centuries by the church as a means of finding unity in the Bible. Each book included in the Bible was measured or evaluated, often after years of debate, in terms of its adequacy for inclusion in the "canon" of authoritative scripture. The primary criterion for inclusion was the book's testimony to God's redemptive purpose, expressed differently over the centuries.

Each of these arguments for unity has limitations, but taken together, they point to a kind of unity or single story in the Bible, especially for those who read with religious convictions. We might say that the unity has been spotted, although described differently. Authors and editors from different eras and cultures and with different languages bear witness to what they understand as the activity of God.[5] The story of the Bible is the story of God's creation, subsequent human failure, God's redemptive activity, and human response. It is a story told in many ways and in different times. From a religious perspective, it is the story of *God's active love for the world.*

Because the story is told so many different ways, the diversity of the Bible is more apparent than its unity.[6] One common story is not always easy to discern because there are so many subplots. In fact there are many "stories" told by a variety of authors and editors, in different times and places, and originally in different languages. The following fundamental and obvious differences illustrate the point:[7]

1. The distinction between the Old Testament and the New Testament.
2. The different languages. The primary language of the Old Testament was Hebrew, and the New Testament was written in Greek, perhaps based in part on some Aramaic sources.
3. The different eras and cultures, spanning nearly fifteen hundred years.
4. The different types of literature, which include history, law, poetry, and doctrine. The Gospels are a nearly unique genre, certainly more than history, and the prophetic and apocalyptic literature is distinctive.
5. The idiosyncratic styles and points of view of the authors and editors of the sixty-six books (excluding the Apocrypha).

The diversity contained within the Bible is part of its richness, but at times when reading the Bible one can appreciate only the tree and not the forest.

Because of the rich diversity contained between the covers of the Bible, one cannot describe the character and style of the Bible as if there were a single author writing from the perspective of one culture and using one language. Nonetheless some attempt to characterize it may be helpful:[8]

1. It is an extremely *complex* book, one removed from us by centuries, other cultures, and different languages. Many of its ideas and categories are not only complex and subtle but embodied in the customs and idioms of the time in which they were expressed. Much in the Bible is expressed in a straightforward manner, and the fundamental plot of the larger story, God's active love for world, can be grasped by all. But there are parts nearly out of our reach, given our distance from the time and culture in which they were written.

2. With some exceptions, the *language of the Bible is eloquent, lively, and concrete.* It abounds in figures of speech and in metaphor and symbol, and illustrations are often drawn from common human experience and the world of nature. It is a rare and beautiful collection of writing.

3. The authors and editors of the Bible have a *broad range of styles.* They write about the breadth of human experience, drawing upon nearly every mode of written communication with which we are familiar. The Bible requires of its readers a sensitivity to the many modes of written communication.

4. The biblical authors and editors, of necessity, speak in *anthropomorphic and analogical language* about many subjects and especially the divine. There are few if any philosophical treatises in the Bible. To make a point, the writers often used images, metaphors, and allegories rather than philosophical discourse. To fully grasp the Bible's "storyline," one must be conversant with the lyric character of the Bible.

5. The Bible grapples in its own unique way with all the *"big questions"* that haunt us in our more reflective moments. Who is God? How does one relate to God? What is the meaning of my life? How should I live my life? Why do we suffer? Is there life after death? It is the Bible's reflection on these subjects that brings us back to its pages again and again.

The Place of the Bible in the Religious Community

The church has thought a great deal about the Bible as a guide for faith and practice. In its theological reflection, the church has not always arrived at consensus on the Bible's role. But as we think about the Bible's place within the church, the following categories, used widely across the church's many traditions, may be helpful.[9]

1. *Revelation:* Christianity, and indeed all three "religions of the Book" (the others are Judaism and Islam) have maintained that humankind could not fully know the divine apart from God's self-disclosure. What is needed is a revelation from God, a word, as it were, from the upper story. The Bible has been understood as a record of God's self-revelation, and therefore intimately connected to the revelation, or, as some would argue, an integral part of the revelation. At the very least, the Bible in Christian understanding is a human record of the observation and experience of the revelation of God.

2. *Word of God:* What is revealed in God's self-disclosure is the divine character and the divine will for the human family. The Bible, as the record of God's revelation, becomes the Word of God. Some argue that every "jot and tittle" is the Word of God; others see the Bible as the human witness of God's revelation, which therefore points to the Word of God that is Jesus Christ. In one way or another, most Christian communities affirm that the Bible contains the Word of God.

3. *Inspiration:* Inevitably, the question arises about the trustworthiness of the Bible. Is what the Bible says accurate and true? Christians have generally turned to the idea of God's inspiration (2 Tim. 3:16) in order to maintain the truthfulness of the biblical witness. The Bible, Christians have argued, in some sense, is inspired by God and therefore trustworthy.

4. *Authority:* If the Bible is an accurate recording of God's revelation, then it becomes authoritative for the community of faith. As the community of faith struggles with complex issues and attempts to guide individual Christians, it turns first to the Bible. The level of authority ascribed to the Bible varies among Christian traditions.[10]

5. *Interpretation:* It is one thing to say the Bible is the inspired Word of God with authority on matters of faith and practice. It is quite another to interpret the Bible's meaning and apply it to contemporary issues and questions. Biblical interpretation is not easy, and a high-quality interpretive effort often requires some training and care.[11]

6. *Tradition:* As we read the Bible, we do so out of our own frame of reference, a cultural, theological, and ecclesiastical tradition. Our tradition gives color to the sunglasses through which we view the Bible. And as we begin to get below the surface in our study of the Bible, we discover that the Bible, both Old and New Testaments, is

layered with tradition. It is out of our tradition that we generally "make sense" of the Bible, but the presence of tradition that colors our reading should give us some humility about claiming that our understanding is the only correct understanding of a particular portion of the Bible.

7. *Function:* Less frequently discussed but important is the particular function the Bible has in a religious community. Its function will vary depending upon the amount of authority attributed to it, but for most Christian communions, the Bible serves as (1) the foundation for theology, (2) the source and basis for sermons and worship, (3) the guide for personal and social ethics, (4) a resource for devotion and spiritual nurture, and (5) the norm for mission strategy and goals.

Methods of Bible Study

In many ways the Bible can be a daunting and intimidating book. It is unrealistic to expect it to be clear and meaningful if it is simply pulled from the shelf, opened, and read at random. More often than not, such an approach leaves the reader lost or bored or both. At times, guidance and inspiration can come from random reading, but the better part of wisdom suggests a more systematic approach to reading the Bible.

There are many approaches to and methods of Bible study, and the choice will depend mainly on the purpose of the study. If it is the mastery of facts in order to pass an ordination exam, certain methods will be better. If it is inspiration and spiritual sustenance, other methods will be better. One way of sorting out the various approaches and methods of study is based on the three worlds into which we are drawn as we read: literary, historical, and contemporary.[12] Each of these worlds has methods of study appropriate to the characteristics of these worlds.

When reading the Bible as literature, you might employ a range of technical approaches such as rhetorical criticism or structuralism,[13] but it is not necessary to become a scholar to understand the literary character of the Bible and appreciate the fact that the Bible is a literary masterpiece. A good starting point is to determine what type of literature you are reading. Is it a myth or legend, such as the profound story of the beginning of time in the earliest chapters of Genesis? Or is it an extended sermon, such as a section from the Gospel of John, that draws upon fact and meaning? As I have said, the Bible contains many types of literature (story, history, poetry, sermon, epistle, apocalyptic vision, etc.), and an awareness of the unique features of each type of literature you encounter will obviously help you understand it. A second step in the literary study of the Bible is to be sensitive to the language of the text. This is particularly important when you read the Bible in translation and are thereby removed from the biblical language. You will discover, for instance, that the language of poetry is quite different from that found in an extended prose passage. You should be especially mindful that images and metaphors are used extensively in poetry, for example. A third step is to identify the major themes being developed by the author. What is the author trying to say, and how is the material organized in order to communicate the point? A fourth step is to analyze the structures of the text and the author's assumptions that undergird the text. The insight gained from these four steps should enable you to fully appreciate the meaning and quality of the writing.

The historical study of the Bible has two dimensions: first, the study of how the Bible came together as a book; second, the study of the history in and around the events recorded in the Bible. The two dimensions are interwoven, but for the sake of clarity, we separate them. The study of the development of the Bible has spawned a number of historical inquiries. They might be summarized as follows:

1. In *tradition criticism* one seeks to uncover how an initial event or utterance has been passed down in oral form and adapted to meet the needs of the religious community. Paul, for example, makes use of the oral tradition on the communion service in 1 Corinthians 11.
2. In *form criticism* one determines the type or form of literature which is being studied, and then attempts to uncover the particular life situation in which the form took shape. The assumption is that the social environment shapes the type and use of the literature.
3. In *source criticism* one attempts to determine what sources were used by an author or editor in the writing of the particular section of the Bible being studied. For example, most scholars accept the view that several sources or documents (the documentary hypothesis) stand behind the Pentateuch.
4. In *redaction criticism* one assumes that much of the literature of the Bible was shaped by editors who combined several sources and then composed the book, often inserting their own particular theme or point of view. Mark and Matthew, for example, may have had access to the same material, but each gave the material a slightly different slant in order to address the particular concerns of his reading audience.
5. In *textual criticism* one reviews the many available editions of the text and attempts to determine which text is the oldest. The oldest text usually is assumed to be closest to the original.

All modes of "criticism" are attempts to reconstruct the development of the Bible, and in so doing, to view the history that stands behind the formation of the Bible. It is a very important effort if, for example, one believes that access to the historical Jesus is possible only through these various types of historical study.

The other dimension of the historical study of the Bible is to research the "world" that surrounded the events recorded in the Bible. Information about the customs and cultures in which the events of the Bible took place add greatly to our understanding of the Bible. What does is mean, for example, for our understanding of the book of Acts or Romans, to know that Paul was a Roman citizen? For Old Testament study, the findings of archaeology have helped shed light on the cultures in which the Bible events occurred.

A third world into which we are drawn as we study the Bible is our contemporary world. Most people who view the Bible as scripture, guiding them and their religious community in matters of faith and practice, view it as a contemporary document. For those of us who understand the Bible in this way, personal study of the Bible amounts to reading it with care, frequently in a small group, and applying the Bible's teaching to our lives. In addition to this simple approach, more sophisticated methodologies and theories have been advanced. One, emphasizing the reader's engagement with the text, stresses that the real meaning of the passage is not available primarily through literary or historical study, but emerges in the reading experience. The experience of the reader supplies the missing elements in the text and provides a more complete meaning to the text.

Still another approach, often referred to as deconstruction, finds fault with "methodology" in general, and emphasizes the reader's creative encounter with the literature. Deconstructionists are also inclined to pull apart or deconstruct a particular method or interpretation in an effort to find the hidden assumptions and motivations, ones that could easily distort the text.

Another contemporary strategy in reading the Bible is to be quite clear about one's point of view and to interpret the text out of this frame of reference. Feminist, liberation, and political motifs are quite common in the current dialogue. And, as has been suggested, religious communities use the Bible for religious purposes—for theological, devotional, ethical, and liturgical reasons.

The study of the Bible, thoughtfully and carefully undertaken by wise and scholarly people for centuries, has produced a vast literature of commentary, numerous study approaches, and a range of interpretive strategies. The preceding orientation is merely suggestive of this corpus of knowledge; it does give us a footing on which to start. We begin with the Pentateuch and with the book of Genesis in particular.

PART TWO

THE HEBREW BIBLE
(THE OLD TESTAMENT)

3

The Pentateuch

The first five books of the Hebrew Bible are often called the Law of Moses (Torah) and referred to as the Pentateuch. They are an integral part of the larger story of the Bible, in many ways laying the foundations for the whole Bible. This body of literature has great variety and quite distinct subsections—which raises the question of how this extraordinary composition was produced. Two theories have been put forward. One argues that the composition is a product of one author who reworked earlier sources into a new piece of literature. The second maintains that a redactor or several redactors edited the material, producing a single text.

Nearly all scholars agree, regardless of their view of the Pentateuch's development, that it is a product of earlier sources. The dominant point of view is the "documentary hypothesis," which posits four primary sources: J (known as J or Yahweh), an early Judean source; E (Elohist), an early north Israelite source; D, the core of Deuteronomy; and P (Priestly), a later source dated near or after the Babylonian exile. The documentary hypothesis is sometimes referred to as JEDP.[1]

Genesis

However the Pentateuch came to us, it starts appropriately with beginnings. Genesis is the narrative account of the beginning of the world, the people of Israel, and the community of faith. In many ways, it is a theological affirmation that Yahweh, the God of Israel, created all that is.

WHO? The story of beginnings is filled with interesting characters who embody the great themes of the writing. Central to the story are these people:

Abel	second son of Adam	4:1–16
Abraham	Hebrew patriarch	12:1–25:18
Adam	first human	1—2
Benjamin	Jacob's last son	35
Cain	first son of Adam and Eve	4
Enoch	seventh patriarch	5
Esau	older son of Isaac	25—36

Eve	first woman	2
Ham	Noah's second son	9
Isaac	second patriarch	21
Jacob	son of Isaac	27
Japheth	son of Noah	9
Joseph	son of Rachel and Jacob	37—50
Levi	third son of Jacob	29:34
Lot	nephew of Abraham	11:31
Methuselah	oldest person in the Bible	5:21–27
Noah	survivor of flood	6—9
Potiphar and wife	Egyptians	39:6–20
Rachel	wife of Jacob	28
Rebekah	wife of Isaac	24
Sarah	matriarch and wife of Abraham	12—23
Shem	eldest son of Noah	6

WHAT? Genesis has four major stories, progressively unfolding with increasing detail, and culminating in the formation of Israel in Egypt.

I.	Primordial history: Story of creation and history of the nations	1—12
II.	Story of Abraham and Sarah	12:1–25:18
III.	Story of Isaac and Jacob	25:19–36:43
IV.	Story of Joseph and his brothers	37:1–50:26

Key Events:

The creation	1:1–2:25
The flood	4:17–6:4
The tower of Babel	11
The travels of Abraham and Sarah	12
The Abrahamic covenant	12
The sacrifice of Isaac	22
Joseph to Egypt	37

WHERE? The events described in Genesis took place in the larger context of the ancient Near East and in ancient Palestine. (See Appendix B, figs. 1 and 2.)

Places to Note:

Assyria	Jerusalem
Babylon	Jordan River
Bethel	Mesopotamia
Dead Sea	Nineveh
Eden	Palestine (Canaan)

Egypt	Persia
Euphrates River	Tigris River
Fertile Crescent	Ur

WHEN? The dates of the several events described in Genesis are disputed, but most scholars would place the events of the Ancestral Period from around 1750 to 1500 B.C.E., although others would place these events from about 1500 to 1200 B.C.E.

WHY? The stories of Genesis were told to explain why the world was created and how the nation of Israel was formed.

As Genesis ends, the people of Israel are a people with an identity, with emerging traditions, and a sense of community. But they remain enslaved in Egypt and await liberation.

Exodus

Genesis ends with the story of the death of Joseph and his burial in Egypt. With his death came the loss of an advocate for the Israelites in the court of Pharaoh: "Now a new king arose over Egypt, who did not know Joseph" (Ex. 1:18). The people are enslaved, and the stage is set for the life and work of Moses.

WHO? The book of Exodus is dominated by the extraordinary presence of Moses. Other important characters are as follows:

Aaron	brother of Moses and Miriam	Exodus 1—40
Rameses	Egyptian pharaoh	
Rameses II	Egyptian pharaoh	

WHAT? Exodus is the account of Moses' call by God to rescue the Israelites from oppression in Egypt. The story takes shape in the following sections.

I.	The oppression	1:1–22
II.	The preparation of Moses for his mission	2:1–7:7
III.	The conflict with Pharaoh	7:8–12:32
IV.	The exodus from Egypt	12:33–15:21
V.	The wilderness wandering	15:22–18:27
VI.	The formation of the community	19:1–40:38

Key Events:

Birth of Moses	2:1–10
Flight to Midian	2:11–15
Burning bush	3:1–12

Moses' return to Egypt	4:18–31
The plagues	7:8–12:32
The passover	12:1–13
The escape from Egypt	14
The Ten Commandments	20:1–17

WHERE? The events described in the book of Exodus took place in Egypt and Canaan. (See Appendix B, fig. 3.)

WHEN? The dates of the exodus are debated, but many scholars date the final exodus from Egypt in the reign of Rameses II (about 1290 B.C.E.). (See Appendix B, fig. 4, to place the exodus in historical context.)

WHY? The book of Exodus was written to describe Israel's formation as a community based upon a covenant with God. The pivotal event, God's liberation in the exodus, gives God "the right" to expect Israel's obedience to the covenant obligations.

Leviticus

As Israel became a community of faith, many religious ceremonies and rituals developed, overseen by the priests. The book of Leviticus records this development and describes the appropriate style of life and worship expected by God in the Israelite community of faith.

WHO? As the Old Testament narrative continues, we see Moses playing a key role in establishing priestly laws and Aaron, the brother of Moses, becoming the central figure in the priestly responsibility. Other actors in the story include the following:

Abihu	son of Aaron	10
Eleazar	son of Aaron	10
Ithamar	son of Aaron	10
Nadab	son of Aaron	10

WHAT? Leviticus is a collection of legal and liturgical material containing instructions for worship and ethical purity. The priestly class, called the Levites, carry out the ritual in the Tabernacle, where God is present. Leviticus may be outlined as follows:

I.	Sacrifices of the people	1:1–7:38
II.	Consecration of Aaron	8:1–10:20
III.	Laws of purity	11:1–15:33
IV.	Laws of holiness	16:1–27:34

WHERE? The laws and regulations presuppose the journey to Canaan, and therefore can be placed in the context of the journey. But rules on circumcision and diet are from a later period.

WHEN? The narrative places Moses and Aaron at the center, but the major portion of the priestly code was more likely developed in the sixth and fifth centuries B.C.E., or even later.

WHY? Leviticus gives quite specific instructions for worship and behavior for the community of faith. As the people of Israel are obedient to the codes, they preserve their identity and legacy and secure the blessing of God.

The Israelites were not consistently obedient to the law of God and were required to "wander" in the wilderness for forty years. Only after the older generation had died would the new generation be allowed to enter the Promised Land.

Numbers

The major theme of Numbers is Yahweh's judgment on the Israelites because of their disobedience and lack of gratitude.

WHO? The older generation fails to meet Yahweh's standards and are deprived of the blessings promised to Abraham. The central characters in addition to Moses and Aaron are as follows:

Balaam	non-Israelite prophet	22:1–24:25
Balak	king of Moab	22 and 23
Caleb	spy sent to Promised Land	14
Joshua	Moses' successor	27
Miriam	sister of Moses and Aaron	12

WHAT? Numbers recounts the Israelites' unfaithfulness, the subsequent wilderness experience, and the preparation for the entrance into Canaan. The story has the following dimensions:

I.	Preparing for the journey to Canaan	1:1–9:23
	A. The census	1:1–4:49
	B. The preparations	5:1–9:23
II.	The journey	10:1–21:20
	A. The departure	10:1–14:45
	B. The desert experiences	15:1–21:20
III.	The events of the journey	21:21–36:13
	A. The battles and victories	21:21–31:53
	B. On the edge of the Promised Land	32:1–36:13

WHERE? The events described, although mixed with material from later sources, occur in the journey of the Israelites from Mount Sinai to the plains of Moab and Transjordan.

WHEN? The many parts of the book of Numbers come from diverse traditions and eras in Israel's history. The book in its present form comes from a period much later than the events recorded.

WHY? Numbers describes all the difficulties encountered by the Israelites in their long journey through the wilderness to Canaan. It underlines the expectations of God and the consequent judgment if those expectations are not met.

The Israelites are now ready to enter the Promised Land.

Deuteronomy

The fifth and final book of the Pentateuch is structured around three speeches of Moses, given to the new generation as they wait in Moab and prepare to cross the Jordan and enter Canaan.

WHO? Once again, the primary characters are those whom we have met before, Moses and Joshua. Others in the story include the following:

Og	king of Basham	3:1–13
Sihon	king of the Amorites	2:24–37

WHAT? Deuteronomy, while reflecting an earlier tradition, presents guidelines for meeting the political problems of the people of Israel in the seventh century B.C.E. It is built around the three farewell speeches of Moses and includes his final days and death. The outline is as follows:

I.	The first address	1:1–4:43
II.	The law of Moses	4:44–26:19
III.	The third speech: On obedience	27:1–30:20
IV.	Moses' final words and death	31:1–34:12

Key Events/Sections:

The Ten Commandments	4:44–5:22
The Shema	6:4–9
The Song of Moses	31:30–32:47
The account of Moses' death	34:1–12

WHERE? The setting is the plain of Moab, anticipating entrance into the land "flowing with milk and honey."

WHEN? Most scholars agree that the Book of the Law, found in 621 B.C.E. when Temple repairs were underway in the time of King Josiah, was the heart of Deuteronomy. The book had great importance during the reign of Josiah, but it represents sources from approximately two hundred years earlier. The first writers may have been from the Northern Kingdom of Israel who were appealing to the Mosaic tradition in order to secure social order.

WHY? Deuteronomy is hortatory in style and calls upon its readers, using the rhetorical device of Moses' speeches, to obey God and receive the divine blessing. The emphasis is on remembrance of what God has done for the people of Israel. Out of gratitude, the people should act ethically, live justly, and care for one another in a neighborly way.

The death of Moses concludes the first section of the Old Testament, but the narrative continues in the historical books.

4

The Prophets

Scholars have suggested many ways to group the books of the Bible. Earlier generations of Christian scholars, following the placement of the books in the Bible, often used the categories of Pentateuch, historical books, wisdom literature, and Prophets. More recent scholarship, as well as the canonical Hebrew Bible, suggests some revision of these categories based on the traditional Hebrew arrangement and historical factors. We will follow the traditional Jewish categories.

THE FORMER PROPHETS

We turn first to the Prophets, separating them into the subcategories of former and latter Prophets. The former Prophets material, in Joshua through 2 Kings, gives a mostly historical account of Israel from the entrance into Canaan (late thirteenth century B.C.E.) to the Babylonian exile (sixth century B.C.E.). The former Prophets books provide the historical context for the latter Prophets books, which reflect on the religious and political history of the people of Israel.

The former Prophets books trace seven critical periods in the history of ancient Israel:[1]

1. The conquest of Canaan (Joshua)
2. The formation of the twelve-tribe confederacy (Judges)
3. The Philistine threat, leading to the establishment of the monarchy (1 and 2 Samuel, 1 Kings)
4. The division of the kingdom into Judah and Israel (1 Kings)
5. The parallel histories with the fall of Israel to Assyria in 721 B.C.E. (2 Kings)
6. King Josiah's reforms in Judah (621 B.C.E.)
7. Babylon's destruction of Judah (587 B.C.E.)

Joshua

The book of Joshua picks up the Bible's story from the Pentateuch. It begins with the death of Moses, who dies in Moab within sight of the

Promised Land. To Joshua, who succeeds Moses, is left the responsibility of leading Israel across the Jordan into Canaan.

WHO? Joshua plays the key role in the conquest of Canaan, but one other character, Rahab the harlot, plays an interesting part as the one who provides shelter for Joshua's party when they come to spy on Jericho (Joshua 2 and 6).

WHAT? The account of Joshua's activity is told as follows:

I.	The transfer of leadership	1:1–5:15
II.	The conquest of Canaan	6:1–12:24
III.	Dividing the territory	13:1–21:45
IV.	Concluding speech and events	22:1–24:33

Key Events:

Spies sent to Jericho	2
Israel crosses the Jordon	3
Jericho conquest	6
The kingdom of Ai captured	8
The sun stands still	10
Joshua's farewell speech	23

WHERE? The events recorded in Joshua take place in Canaan. Other locations to note are as follows:

Ai	Gilgal	Jordon River
Gibeon	Jericho	Shechem

WHEN? Most scholars place the entrance into Canaan at about 1250 B.C.E. The book of Joshua, most likely a part of a larger work called the Deuteronomistic History, was probably written in the late seventh century B.C.E.

WHY? The book of Joshua was written to record a crucial period of Israel's history and to remind the people of Israel that the word of Yahweh is heard in the events of Israel's history. Yahweh's will can be discovered in the word but also in the event, if one is spiritually sensitive enough to discern the divine plan in the course of actions and events. The book of Joshua also raises the problem of the divine sanction of war and conquest.

Judges

The book of Judges describes the transitional period between Joshua's death and the establishment of the monarchy and underlines the gradual historical process that constituted the so-called conquest of Canaan, the area also called Palestine. The gradual infiltration may be viewed as a struggle between the religion of Israel and the religion of Canaan.

WHO? Several leaders arise to give order to the Israelite's settlement in Canaan. Important names to remember are as follows:

Abimelech	local king	8:31
Baal	Canaanite god	8:33
Barak	commander of Israelite militia	4:4–9
Deborah	judge and prophet	4—5
Delilah	woman who loved Samson	16:4–22
Gideon	major judge	6:11–8:32
Nazirites	strict religious sect	13:1–7
Philistines	seafaring people in Canaan	3:1–3
Samson	Israelite hero	13:1–25

WHAT? After a brief introduction, the book of Judges recounts the strong leadership and exploits of several military leaders. However, social order remains elusive as does religious purity. The book may be outlined as follows:

I.	Introduction expressing the troubled times	1:1–3:6
II.	The charismatic leaders	3:7–16:31
III.	Lessons from the past	17:1–21:25

Key Events:

Deborah's song	5
Gideon's leadership	6—8
Abimelech's monarchy	9
Samson's story	13—16

WHERE? The events recorded in the book of Judges take place in Palestine. (See Appendix B, fig. 5.)

WHEN? The events occur between approximately 1200 and 1020 B.C.E. The stories of the period were most likely collected during the monarchy, edited in the late seventh century B.C.E., and then reedited after the destruction of Jerusalem (587 B.C.E.).

WHY? The book of Judges describes a time in the life of Israel when the social order was limited, and unfaithfulness and conflict prevailed. The book of Judges partially attributes the social and political problems to Israel's failure to keep the covenant, causing Yahweh to desert Israel and deliver its people over to their enemies. Toward the end of the book is the lament, "In those days there was no king of Israel, and every man did as he pleased" (Judg. 21:25).

1 Samuel

The founding and formation of the Israelite monarchy are related in 1 Samuel. The dominant point of view in the account is theological and ascribes to Yahweh interventions in Israel's affairs.

WHO? Several important biblical characters are introduced in 1 Samuel:

David	king of Israel	1—31
Eli	judge of Israel	4
Goliath	Philistine warrior	17
Hannah	mother of Samuel	1
Jonathan	son of Saul	13—14
Michal	David's wife	18
Samuel	prophet	1—31
Saul	first king of Israel	9

WHAT? The book of 1 Samuel, with 2 Samuel, describes the rise of the kingship in Israel and records the life of David. Its contents may be outlined as follows:

I.	The story of Samuel	1:1–7:17
II.	The election and rejection of Saul	8:1–16:13
III.	The rise of David	16:14–31:13

Key Events:

The ark narrative	4:1–7:1
Saul's election	9:1–11:15
The anointing of David	16:1–13
The battle with Goliath	17

WHERE? The events described take place in Israel and Philistia. (See Appendix B, fig. 6.)

WHEN? The rise of the kingship in Israel occurs in the eleventh century B.C.E. The books of 1 and 2 Samuel are part of the Deuteronomistic History, which evolves into its finished form at the time of the exile (sixth century B.C.E.) or slightly earlier.

WHY? The books of 1 and 2 Samuel are written from the perspective of divine election. It is God who intervenes in Samuel's conception, who appoints him as kingmaker and kingbreaker, and who anoints Saul and David.

2 Samuel

The book of 2 Samuel picks up the story of David and recounts his life, problems, and reign as king of Israel.

WHO? David is the key player in 2 Samuel, but he has several teammates. Among them are the following:

Abner	army commander	2
Absalom	son of David	13—20
Amnon	eldest son of David	13
Bathsheba	consort of David's	11
Joab	arm commander	8
Nathan	prophet	7, 12
Solomon	son of David, king	12
Tamar	daughter of David	13
Uriah	warrior and husband of Bathsheba	11

WHAT? Second Samuel describes the reign of King David, his military victories, and the founding of the capital. It also is an account of David's mistakes and the consequences of those mistakes. The book may be outlined as follows:

I.	David becomes king	1:1–5:10
II.	The reign of David	5:11–20:22
III.	Last words	21:1–24:25

Key Events:

David anointed king	2
Jerusalem made capital	5
Ark brought to Jerusalem	6
Covenant with David	7
David commits adultery	11
Absalom's tragic story	14—18

WHERE? The events described in 2 Samuel occur in Israel. (See Appendix B, fig. 6.)

WHEN? David reigns in the eleventh century B.C.E.

WHY? The book, like 1 Samuel, describes God's guiding hand in the affairs of Israel.

1 Kings

The books of 1 and 2 Kings were considered one book in Jewish tradition. They provide the major history of the Israelite monarchy, covering the four centuries from the death of David and the succession of Solomon (ca. 965 B.C.E.) until the destruction of Jerusalem and the exile (587 B.C.E.). First Kings deals primarily with the reign of Solomon and then describes events leading to the divided monarchy.

WHO? Solomon is the leading character in the narrative, but he is surrounded by others, including the following:

Ahab	ruler over Israel	16
Asa	ruler over Judah	15
Elijah	prophet	17, 18
Jehoshaphat	ruler over Judah	22
Jeroboam	rebel and ruler	11, 12
Jezebel	wife of Ahab	16
Queen of Sheba	ruler of Sabaens	20
Rehoboam	son of Solomon, king	12—14

(See Appendix B, fig. 4.)

WHAT? The story of 1 Kings opens with the death of David and then proceeds to Solomon's succession. Solomon is pictured as wise and ambitious, but he mistakenly tolerates foreign cults, which leads to the breakup of the kingdom. The rest of the book tells of the successive kings of the divided kingdom of Judah and Israel. The book unfolds in two major categories:

I.	The reign of Solomon	1:1–11:43
II.	The divided monarchy	12:1–22:51

Key Events:

The ascension of Solomon	1
The death of David	2
Solomon's wisdom	3
The building of the Temple	6
The visit of the Queen of Sheba	10
The northern tribe secedes	12

Jeroboam I's reign in Israel	12
Rehoboam reigns in Judah	14
Ahab reigns over Israel	16
Elijah's ministry	17—19

WHERE? The events recorded in 1 Kings take place in Palestine. Under Solomon, there is a united kingdom, but upon his death, the kingdom divides into a northern region (Israel) and a southern region (Judah).

WHEN? First Kings describes the forty years of Solomon's reign in the tenth century B.C.E., and then records the reign of the rulers of the kingdoms of Israel and Judah in the mid-ninth century B.C.E. The final version of 1 Kings, as part of a larger history, probably dates from about 550 B.C.E., although the authors/editors draw upon earlier sources.

WHY? The point of view in 1 and 2 Kings, following the Deuteronomistic historians, is that violators of God's law and worship expectations will be punished. Yahweh permits Jerusalem's fall and the end of David's royal house because of disobedience. The conflict between Elijah and Ahab epitomizes the theme.

2 Kings

The book of 2 Kings continues the historical narrative. It argues that the destruction of Israel, which fell to the Assyrians in 721 B.C.E., and Judah, which was defeated by Babylon in 587 B.C.E., is the product of disobedience.

WHO? Several important characters in the narrative include these names:

Ahaziah	ruler over Judah	1
Elisha	prophet	2
Hezekiah	ruler over Judah	18
Jehoram	ruler of Israel	3
Jehu	ruler of Israel	9
Josiah	ruler of Judah	22
Manasseh	ruler of Judah	21
Nebuchadnezzar	ruler of Babylonia	25
Sennacherib	Assyrian king	18

(See Appendix B, fig. 4.)

WHAT? The story of 2 Kings has the following structure:

I.	The ministry of Elisha	1:1–8:29
II.	Trouble in Israel	9:1–14:29

III. Last days of Israel	15:1–18:12
IV. The kingdom of Judah	18:13–25:30

Key Events:

Elijah ascends to heaven	2
Elisha succeeds Elijah	2
Israel carried captive to Assyria	17
Josiah's reign over Judah	22, 23
Fall and captivity of Judah	25

WHERE? The events took place in Palestine, with references to Assyria and Babylonia.

WHEN? Second Kings narrates the story of the divided kingdom from approximately 850 B.C.E. until the Babylonian captivity (587 B.C.E.).

WHY? Second Kings offers a theological interpretation of the events that led to the fall of the kings of Israel and Judah.

THE LATTER PROPHETS

With the closing of 2 Kings, we complete our discussion of the writings of the former Prophets, which provide a historical account of Israel's history from the movement into Canaan to the collapse of Judah. The latter Prophets, often divided into major and minor prophets, reflect on this period of history.

The terms "major" and "minor" reflect the size of the writings, not their importance. In the traditional Hebrew canon, the major prophets are Isaiah, Jeremiah, and Ezekiel; the Book of Twelve constitutes the minor prophets. Daniel is included among the Writings, and we will discuss Daniel in that section.

Prophets in Israel were persons who were "called to announce." They interpreted the events of history in light of God's intentions and attempted to keep alive the memory of the exodus. Their message took the form of interpreting the faith of Israel for the contemporary situation and proclaiming God's will during national crises. Later, after the fall of Israel and Judah, they often spoke words of comfort and hope.

Since prophetic books do not appear in the Bible in chronological order, a listing of the times of their writing and ministry may be helpful.

Eighth Century:

Amos (ca. 750 B.C.E.)
Hosea (ca. 740 B.C.E.)

Isaiah of Jerusalem (ca. 742–701 B.C.E.)
Micah (ca. 725 B.C.E.)

Seventh Century:

Zephaniah (ca. 640–609 B.C.E.)
Naham (ca. 612 B.C.E.)
Habakkuk (ca. 600 B.C.E.)

Sixth Century:

Jeremiah (ca. 620–587 B.C.E.)
Ezekiel (ca. 590 B.C.E.)
Obadiah (ca. 587 B.C.E.)
Second Isaiah (ca. 550–539 B.C.E.)
Haggai (ca. 530 B.C.E.)
Zechariah (ca. 520 B.C.E.)

Late Sixth or Fifth Century:

Joel (date uncertain)
Malachi (date uncertain)
Jonah (date uncertain)

Isaiah

The book of Isaiah is a collection of Hebrew writing, likely stretching from the mid-seventh to the fifth century B.C.E. Scholars often divide the writing into three separate books, Isaiah of Jerusalem (1—39), Second Isaiah (40—55), and Third Isaiah (56—66).

WHO? The three authors are of note: Isaiah of Jerusalem, an anonymous poet in Babylonia who wrote Second Isaiah, and the prophet in postexilic Judah who wrote Third Isaiah.

WHAT? Isaiah interprets two major historical crises—the war with Syria (734 B.C.E.) and the Assyrian threats (734–701 B.C.E.)—as expressions of God's sovereignty over history and divine judgment of social injustice. The latter sections of the book of Isaiah address themes of judgment and restoration at the end of the exile. The book breaks naturally into the three sections.

Key Passages:

Isaiah's call	6
The peaceful kingdom	11
The suffering servant	52—53

WHERE? The events upon which Isaiah of Jerusalem reflects occur in Judah. Other sections of Isaiah are reflections on the events of the exile in Babylon and the return to Jerusalem.

WHEN? Isaiah of Jerusalem writes in the second half of the eighth century between 740 and 701 B.C.E. The current form of the book appeared in the second century B.C.E. Second Isaiah was probably written between 547 and 539 B.C.E. and Third Isaiah about 520 B.C.E.

WHY? Isaiah of Jerusalem ponders the theological meaning of the historical events of his time, denounces greed and disregard for the poor, urges reliance upon Yahweh, and predicts a time of peace and justice. Similar themes recur in the other two sections of Isaiah, but point specifically to conditions of the time in which these authors write.

Jeremiah

The prophet Jeremiah had a long career, and his specific message changed with changing circumstances. But themes of divine judgment against a covenant-breaking Judah recur.

WHO? Again, familiar names appear, such as the kings of Judah. But Jeremiah's powerful personality and prophetic message to Judah dominate the book.

WHAT? The book may be divided into three major sections, with a final historical appendix.

I.	Visions and prophecies of judgment	1—24
II.	Personal stories and laments	25—45
III.	Prophecies against the nations	46—51
IV.	Historical appendix	52

Key Passages:

The Babylonian captivity foretold	25
The new covenant	31

WHERE? The primary events of the book occur in Judah, but these events were shaped by the religion and politics of the wider region. (See Appendix B, fig. 7.)

WHEN? Jeremiah's career extends from 627 to 586 B.C.E., and the book reflects upon the events in Judah over this period. The book's current form includes editing by later disciples.

WHY? The heart of Jeremiah's message is that Yahweh will crush Judah for abandoning the covenant, and that Babylon is God's chosen means of judgment.

Ezekiel

Ezekiel, like Jeremiah, preaches a message of judgment and doom, but emphasizes as well that God will not forsake the people of Judah. The themes of salvation and hope are clearly present.

WHO? Ezekiel is a younger contemporary of Jeremiah who was taken to Babylon when King Nebuchadnezzar captured Jerusalem in 587 B.C.E.

WHAT? This book has a threefold structure. Its special quality is the use of unusual visions and symbols.

I.	Oracles of judgment against Jerusalem and Judah	1—24
II.	Oracles against foreign nations	25—32
III.	Prophecies of future restorations	33—52

Key Passages:

Valley of the dry bones	37
Gog and Magog	38—39

WHERE? The events related in Jeremiah occur in Judah and Babylon.

WHEN? These events occur between 627 and 587 B.C.E. The book in its present form is a product of editing by a school of disciples.

WHY? The book was written to proclaim that the Holy God must judge an unholy people, but that God will restore true worship and the new Jerusalem.

Hosea

Hosea is the only native prophet of Israel whose words have survived in a canonical book. He writes about Israel's apostasy, using the metaphor of an unhappy marriage.

WHO? Hosea, the native Israelite prophet, is the main character in the book. Gomer, Hosea's wife and a prostitute, is integral to the story.

WHAT? Hosea compares Israel's unfaithfulness to Yahweh to unfaithfulness in marriage. He urges Israel to return to Yahweh's love. The story is developed in three sections:

I.   Hosea's marriage compared to God's relationship
     to Israel   1—3
II. Consequences of Israel's unfaithfulness to God   4—13
III. Life after judgment   14

WHERE? The prophet writes about events in ancient Israel.

WHEN? The events occur in the last turbulent times of the Northern Kingdom. The book has been edited, with additions such as the postscript in chapter 14.

WHY? Hosea writes about apostasy and judgment, but adds a view of God who suffers over the unfaithfulness of the chosen people.

Joel

The prophet Joel compares a plague of locusts to God's future judgment and speaks of the outpouring of God's spirit on all humanity.

WHO? Joel is a prophet in Judah.

WHAT? Joel writes of judgment and restoration. His message may be understood in the following categories:

I.   National discouragement over the locust plague   1
II. The day of the Lord as judgment on Judah   2:1–29
III. Judgment on Judah's enemies   2:30–3:21

WHERE? The events described by Joel occur in the Southern Kingdom of Judah.

WHEN? These events, the plagues as well as the economic hardship, suggest a date of the early fifth century B.C.E.

WHY? The book was written to stress God's judgment on an unfaithful people, but also to bring comfort by pointing to a new age when the land will recover and God's spirit will be poured out on all humanity.

Amos

In Amos, the theme of judgment is clearly expressed. The last section, promising restoration and peace, may be a later addition.

WHO? Amos, an older contemporary of Hosea, was a prophet from Judah who spoke of God's judgment on the Northern Kingdom of Israel. His writing became a model for future prophets.

WHAT? The theme of judgment is developed as follows:

I. Oracle of judgment against the nations and Israel   1—6
II. Sermons and visions of judgment   7–9:8
III. Prophecies of salvation   9:9–15

WHERE? The judgments described in Amos are to come on the Northern Kingdom of Israel.

WHEN? Although placed third among the minor prophets, Amos is the first prophet to have his words recorded in book form, about 750 B.C.E.

WHY? The prophet Amos, struggling to understand the events of his day, attributes Israel's problems to the judgment of God, judgment that is provoked by Israel's unfaithfulness.

Obadiah

Obadiah is the shortest book in the Old Testament. Its prophecy is directed against the Edomites for benefiting from Judah's destruction.

WHO? Obadiah is an unknown prophet about whom we have little historical or biographical information. The Edomites, a people living adjacent to Judah, benefit from Judah's troubles.

WHAT? The small book is in three sections:

I. The destruction of Edom   1:1–9
II. The misdeeds of Edom   1:10–14
III. The restoration of Israel   1:15–21

WHERE? Obadiah speaks about events in Judah.

WHEN? The events about which Obadiah speaks occur in the early sixth century after the Babylonian destruction of Jerusalem.

WHY? The prophet echoes the theme of God's active intervention in human affairs, judging evil and promising restoration.

Jonah

Jonah is most likely a parable describing an unknown prophet's reluctance to accept his divine call, and God's power and mercy in human affairs.

WHO? Jonah is an eighth-century Israelite prophet, mentioned in 2 Kings 14:25. Most likely the book was written much later, using the name of the earlier prophet.

WHAT? The book of Jonah may be outlined as follows:

I.	Jonah's call and reluctant reaction	1
II.	Jonah in the great fish	2
III.	Jonah as the preacher of repentance in Nineveh	3:1–4:5
IV.	Jonah and the bush	4:6–11

WHERE? Significant is this book's concern with prophecies in the Assyrian city of Nineveh, a partial break from the usual prophetic pattern of judging Judah or Israel.

WHEN? The book is most likely postexilic and may be dated approximately in the sixth century B.C.E.

WHY? The message of the book is elusive, but it does suggest that Yahweh is not local but universal and cares for the affairs of pagan nations as well as those of the chosen people.

Micah

Micah is a book of prophetic addresses focused on the themes of punishment and salvation.

WHO? Micah is a younger contemporary of Isaiah of Jerusalem.

WHAT? Micah's message is one of divine judgment upon both Israel and Judah. Its predictions of Yahweh's future reign may be editorial additions. Micah, as a country dweller, is especially critical of city life, which is filled with sin and injustice. He has little patience with the Davidic dynasty and Temple cult. The book is structured as follows:

I.	First set of speeches on punishment and salvation	1—5
II.	Second set of speeches on punishment and salvation	6—7

WHERE? The prophecy concerns both Israel and Judah.

WHEN? The first verse dates Micah in the reign of Hezekiah in the last decade of the eighth century B.C.E. As with most of the prophets, there are later additions.

WHY? Micah is concerned about true religion, as expressed in 6:8: "He has told you, O mortal, what is good; and what does the LORD require of you but to do justice, and to love kindness, and to walk humbly with your God?"

Nahum

Nahum, unlike the other prophets, limits his remarks to rejoicing over Nineveh's fall.

WHO? It is likely that Nahum functioned as a prophet in the Temple in Jerusalem.

WHAT? Nahum writes of Yahweh's judgment of Assyrian inhumanity. His writing may be outlined as follows:

I.	The wrath of God	1
II.	The destruction of the wicked city	2—3

WHERE? Nineveh is the capital of Assyria.

WHEN? The book was most likely composed about 612 B.C.E., shortly after the capture of Nineveh by the Medo-Babylonian coalition.

WHY? Nahum moves out of reflections solely upon Israel and Judah and speaks of Yahweh as the universal sovereign God.

Habakkuk

Habakkuk is a small theodicy, a reflection on why God permits the destruction of the people of Israel by unbelieving foreigners.

WHO? Nothing is known about Habakkuk except what can be deduced from his writing.

WHAT? The prophet writes about the coming destruction of Judah by Babylon. The book has the following structure:

I.	The dialogue between God and Habakkuk	1–2:19
II.	Hymn of God's victory	2:20–3:19

WHERE? The events about which Habakkuk writes occur in Judah.

WHEN? The Babylonian armies are threatening Judah, which suggests that Habakkuk was written between 600 and 587 B.C.E.

WHY? Habakkuk raised the profound issue of whether God will bring justice in human affairs. Habakkuk holds to the belief that God will, but wonders "how long" he will have to wait.

Zephaniah

Zephaniah, repeating the theme of Amos, tells of the coming universal judgment of Yahweh. The end of the book deals with forgiveness and restoration, but this section may be the work of a later compiler.

WHO? Zephaniah is a prophet of Judah.

WHAT? He writes about God's judgment on idolatrous practices during the reigns of Manasseh (697–642 B.C.E.) and Ammon (642–640 B.C.E.) in Judah. His work is developed as follows:

I.	The universal judgment in the day of the Lord	1:1–2:4
II.	The vivid pictures of judgment	2:5–3:8
III.	The promise of salvation	3:9–20

WHERE? Zephaniah is concerned primarily with the affairs of Judah but also speaks of universal judgment.

WHEN? He writes during the reign of King Josiah (640–609 B.C.E.).

WHY? Zephaniah speaks about the fire of God's wrath, which will burn up a creation that has gone bad, and issues a call for repentance by Jerusalem and Judah. The central sin is idolatry.

Haggai

Haggai urges the restored community of Jerusalem to rebuild the Temple.

WHO? We know little about the author except what may be discerned from his writing.

WHAT? Haggai argues strongly that the Temple should be rebuilt and both the ruler and the high priest have responsibility. The book is structured as follows:

I.	God's call to rebuild the Temple	1:1–11
II.	The response	1:12–15
III.	The future glory of the Temple	2:1–9
IV.	Promised blessing	2:10–19
V.	God's promise to Zerrubbabel	2:20–23

WHERE? The Temple is to be rebuilt in Jerusalem.

WHEN? The rebuilding of the Temple is to be undertaken by a faithful remnant, which has returned from Babylon. The time is during the reign of Darius I (about 520 B.C.E.).

WHY? Haggai anticipates renewed prosperity and the restoration of the Davidic line of kings. The Temple symbolizes the restoration.

Zechariah

The book of Zechariah is really two books, one written during the time of Haggai and the other written later. Zechariah's theme is similar to that of Haggai, that the Temple must be rebuilt.

WHO? Zechariah is a contemporary of Haggai, and the "Second Zechariah" is an unknown writer reflecting conditions in Judah at a later period.

WHAT? The heart of Zechariah's work is eight visions urging the rebuilding of the Temple.

I. God's word to Zechariah	1:1–7
II. The eight visions	1:8–6:15
III. Zechariah speaks	7—8
IV. The later collection of oracles	9—14

WHERE? The events about which the prophet speaks center on Jerusalem.

WHEN? Zechariah reflects on the return of the exiles to Judah following the edict of Cyrus in 538 B.C.E.

WHY? The theme of restoration is central in the first section of Zechariah. The second section, while difficult to interpret, reflects conditions in the fourth century B.C.E., and has an eschatological and apocalyptic character.

Malachi

Malachi, the last of the books in the Old Testament, urges a dispirited group of Judeans to seek and do God's will. Malachi points toward a messenger who will come (3:1).

WHO? Malachi, meaning "my messenger," may be a reference to the theme of the book, not the name of the author, about whom we know nothing.

WHAT? The message of Malachi is similar to that of the other prophets—divine judgment on disobedience and improper worship. Malachi appeals for repentance and faithfulness to God. It may be outlined as follows:

I.	Opening oracle	1:1–5
II.	Condemnation of corrupt worship	1:6–2:9
III.	The covenant faithlessness of Judah	2:10–16
IV.	God's judgment	2:17–3:5
V.	An appeal for repentance	3:6–12
VI.	God's justice	3:13–4:3
VII.	Remember the Torah	4:4–6

WHERE? The conditions calling forth the prophet's response exist in Judah.

WHEN? The book was probably composed during the reign of Xerxes (486–465 B.C.E.), during the time between the reestablishment of the Temple (515 B.C.E.) and the mission of Nehemiah (445 B.C.E.).

WHY? The author writes to warn of divine judgment and to call the Judeans to repentance and faithful worship of God. If the people of God will respond, a better day will come.

5

The Writings

The third major division of the Hebrew Bible, called the Writings, is the most diversified part of the Bible. It was the final section to be accepted into the canon, after serious discussion and debate by the Jewish community. Several types of literature are found in the collection—poetry and songs, wisdom literature, short stories, historical narrative, and apocalyptic literature. We turn first to wisdom literature.

WISDOM LITERATURE

The origins of the wisdom tradition are unknown but ancient. In the life of ancient Israel, the sage was highly respected and often served as a counselor to royalty. Although sages occasionally rose from the priestly or prophetic classes, they were not limited to these groups. The gift of wisdom was viewed as divine in origin, similar to the gift of the prophetic word. Wisdom was expressed in the Bible in several literary forms, including riddles, fables, and proverbs, as well as sophisticated reflection on the troubling questions of life such as suffering, meaning, and death.

Proverbs

The book of Proverbs contains practical advice drawn from many sources.

WHO? Proverbs is traditionally ascribed to Solomon, who is often thought of as the founder of Israel's wisdom schools, although there are many sources for the collection of wisdom in the book.

WHAT? The book of Proverbs emphasizes practical wisdom, guiding its readers to their appropriate roles in society. The book is organized as follows:

I.	The wisdom poems	1—9
II.	The wisdom sayings	10:1–22:16
III.	Various admonitions	22:17–24:22
IV.	The sayings of the wise	24:23–34

V.	Wise sayings of Solomon	25—27
VI.	Sayings of Agur	30
VII.	The sayings of Lemuel's mother	31:1–9
VIII.	Ode to an ideal wife	31:10–31

WHERE? The wisdom sayings of Proverbs provide advice for the community of ancient Israel.

WHEN? In its present form, Proverbs may be dated in the postexilic period (late sixth century B.C.E.), but many sayings originated early in the monarchy (ca. 1004–926 B.C.E.).

WHY? The book of Proverbs contains practical wisdom and traces of speculative wisdom as well. There are some religious themes, although the wisdom is not necessarily religious in character and is universally applicable.

Job

Job is a literary masterpiece addressing the most profound questions of life. It is the Bible's best example of speculative wisdom and rises above its time of composition to speak to the haunting dilemmas of contemporary life. Its theme is human suffering and evil and the extent to which God is morally bound to protect mortals from unmerited pain. The author does not supply conventional answers but gives an "alternative" way of looking at and living with the problem.

WHO? Job, a blameless man, tested by God, is the central figure in the story. In addition, there are Job's three friends, Eliphaz, Bildad, and Zophar; Elihu, who provides another point of view; and Job's family.

WHAT? Job, the righteous man, caught between Satan and God, has his faith tested. Is he righteous because it "pays" or is his piety disinterested and genuine? Job's protective "hedge" is removed, he is tested, and he remains faithful. The story unfolds in six segments:

I.	The prologue: Job's problem	1—2
II.	Job's opening reflections	3
III.	The cycle of dialogues with friends	4—27
IV.	Job's continuing reflections	28—37
V.	Dialogues with God	38:1–42:6
VI.	The epilogue: Job's restoration	42:7–17

WHERE? The legend may be linked to the ancestral figure named in Ezekiel 14:14, 20, but it is not possible to identify any precise location where the story originated.

WHEN? Scholars have proposed dates ranging from the seventh century to the fourth century B.C.E.

WHY? "Why" is indeed the question of the book. Why do humans experience undeserved suffering? Why doesn't God intervene to relieve the suffering? How is it that humans relate to God in the midst of suffering? Job explores these questions and provides no simple answers apart from the counsel to remain faithful.

Ecclesiastes

This writing explores the futility of human wisdom and effort. It is the Bible's finest expression of skeptical wisdom.

WHO? The book is attributed to Solomon as a literary device, one that is soon dropped in favor of the title *koheleth,* meaning "the preacher" or "one who presides over a congregation."

WHAT? In contrast to the passionate search for answers in Job, Ecclesiastes offers detached reflections on the impossibility of finding meaning in life and the folly of human endeavor. A postscript adds a more positive note. The structure of the philosophical discourse is as follows:

I.	Opening prologue	1:1–11
II.	The vanity of all things	1:12–6:12
III.	Words of wisdom	7:1–12:7
IV.	Epilogue	12:8–14

WHERE? It is not possible to pinpoint the place of writing, but the informal Hebrew suggests a possible Northern location.

WHEN? The language suggests a postexilic date.

WHY? The author attempts to grasp the meaning of human existence, but the answers elude him. Instead, one must go through life recognizing one's limited perspective, acknowledging the limits of wisdom, and finding comfort in "the questions themselves."

POETRY

Another genre represented in the Writings is poetry, which grows out of the music of the worshiping community. Most Hebrew poetry repeats in the second line what was expressed in the preceding line, creating parallelism. Often these poems were sung antiphonally by the congregation.

Psalms

The primary expression of Hebrew poetry is found in the psalms, an anthology of religious poetry. Psalms deal with many subjects, but most address God in some fashion. There are laments, songs of praise, wisdom songs, and songs of blessing and cursing.

WHO? Traditionally, many of the psalms were attributed to David, but modern scholarship suggests that many of the psalms were composed by bards for community worship and private devotion.

WHERE? The psalms served the people of ancient Israel.

WHEN? As a collection, the psalms have no single date, but come from many different periods. The collection reached its current form in post-exilic times.

WHAT? The psalms may be described as liturgical songs, performed in the Temple at the nation's religious ceremonies. The collection is organized in five major sections that have more to do with the age of the psalm than its subject. The sections are as follows:

I	Book I: The oldest psalms	1—41
II.	Book II	42—72
III.	Book III	73—89
IV.	Book IV	90—106
V.	Book V	107—150

WHY? The psalms are poems of beauty, inspiration, devotion, deep feeling, and worship. They represent the spiritual character of life among the people of ancient Israel.

THE FESTIVAL SCROLLS (MEGILLOT)

Five books—Ruth, Song of Solomon, Ecclesiastes, Lamentations, and Esther—were selectively read by the ancient Jewish community on the five most important festival days of religious worship through the year. (We have placed Ecclesiastes within the wisdom section because of its content.)

Ruth

Ruth, associated somewhat arbitrarily with the Feast of Weeks, is placed first among the five because the story is the earliest, "in the days of the Judges." It is the story of a Moabite woman who becomes a follower of Yahweh and the great-grandmother of David.

WHO? Ruth, a loving and loyal Moabite widow, is the character around whom the story revolves. Others in the story include Naomi, who is Ruth's mother-in-law, and Boaz, a relative of Naomi who marries Ruth.

WHAT? The beautiful story has the following structure:

I. Ruth and Naomi	1:1–22
A. Ruth is married and widowed	1:1–5
B. Naomi takes Ruth to Judah	1:6–22
II. Ruth and Boaz	2:1–4:22
A. Ruth in the fields of Boaz	2:1–23
B. Ruth and Boaz at the threshing floor	3:1–18
C. Boaz marries Ruth	4:1–12
D. A son is born	4:13–22

WHERE? The events take place in Moab and Jerusalem.

WHEN? The story may have been written quite early, perhaps sometime between the tenth and eighth centuries B.C.E.

WHY? The story is intended to provide a bridge from the time of the judges to the monarchy and to trace David's antecedents. It is also a statement that a foreigner can be not only a member of the covenant community but an ancestor to the divinely appointed monarch.

Esther

The book of Esther, like the book of Ruth, is one of the festival scrolls in the Hebrew canon (Feast of Purim) and among the historical books in the Christian canon. Both are short stories about faithful and courageous women.

WHO? Esther, as a beautiful Jewish queen, risks her life to save her people from the villain Haman, chief administrator in the Persian court. Others in the story are as follows:

Ahasuerus (Xerxes I)	ruler of the Persian Empire
Mordecai	devout Jew who aids Esther
Vashti	divorced wife of Ahasuerus

WHAT? The story of Esther depicts the plight of Jews scattered across the Persian Empire. Haman plans a mass execution of the Jewish people but is foiled by the work of Mordecai and Esther. The novella unfolds as follows:

I.	The Persian court and king	1
II.	Esther becomes Ahasuerus's queen	2
III.	Haman's promotion and plan to destroy the Jews	3—4
IV.	Haman's plot thwarted	5:1–8:2
V.	The tragedy prevented	8:3–10:3

WHERE? The story is set in the Persian Empire during the reign of Xerxes I. (See Appendix B, fig. 4.)

WHEN? Xerxes I reigned from 486 to 465 B.C.E.

WHY? The story, while not mentioning God, nevertheless describes the brave action of Jews in a foreign land. It clearly depicts the forces of good triumphing over the forces of evil.

Song of Solomon

The Song of Solomon (or Song of Songs) is an anthology of love poems held together by the common theme of erotic love. As a festival scroll, it is associated with the Feast of Passover.

WHO? The book is traditionally attributed to Solomon, probably because of his many marriages. The characters in the poems are a man (called king and shepherd), a woman, and the daughters of Jerusalem.

WHAT? The lyric songs reflect feelings of yearning, admiration, self-assessment, and delight in the charms of the beloved. The poems are organized as follows:

I.	The colloquy of the bride	1:1–8
II.	The colloquy of the groom	1:8–2:7
III.	The celebration of love	2:8–3:11
IV.	The dialogues	4:1–8:4
V.	Homecoming	8:5–14

WHERE? The poems may have been used as part of wedding ceremonies in ancient Israel.

WHEN? The present form of the Song of Solomon is probably postexilic.

WHY? The traditional interpretation of the Song of Solomon by both the synagogue and the church is that it is an allegory of God's love for Israel, and God's love for the church. This interpretation may be defensible, but not at the expense of seeing the songs as expressions of human love.

Lamentations

The book of Lamentations, associated with the fast of Ab (August), is a collection of five dirges, mourning the destruction of Jerusalem.

WHO? Tradition assigns Jeremiah as author, but the book is more likely an anthology of poems by more than one poet.

WHAT? The authors' lament over the destruction of Jerusalem is structured as follows:

I.	The desolate and forsaken city	1
II.	God's warning fulfilled	2
III.	God's steadfast love endures	3
IV.	The punishment of Zion	4
V.	The appeal for the Lord to remember the people's affliction	5

WHERE? The poems are expressions of grief over the destruction of the Temple in Jerusalem by the Babylonians (586 B.C.E.).

WHEN? The book was most likely composed following the destruction of Jerusalem.

WHY? The five poems express the deep anguish of the people of Israel for the loss of their holy city. They regret that their own sin caused Yahweh's harsh judgment and plead for divine mercy.

APOCALYPTIC LITERATURE

Still another genre in the Old Testament, apocalyptic literature, tells the meaning of events that are ordinarily not understood by humankind.

Daniel

The book of Daniel describes a faithful Jew in the court of Nebuchadnezzar, a Jew whose apocalyptic visions encompass the rise and fall of Near Eastern empires.

WHO? Daniel, the faithful Jew and court magician, is divinely delivered from unjust punishments. He is surrounded by three friends, Shadrach, Meshach, and Abednego. In addition, we encounter King Belshazzar, a Babylonian governor, and Nebuchadnezzar, a Babylonian king.

WHAT? The book has two major sections, one describing Daniel's experience in the court of Nebuchadnezzar and the other a series of visions about the ebb and flow of Near Eastern empires. The book may be outlined as follows:

I.	Daniel and friends in the Babylonian court	1—6
	A. The testing	1
	B. Nebuchadnezzar's dream	2
	C. The fiery furnace	3
	D. Nebuchadnezzar's madness	4
	E. Belshazzar's feast	5
	F. The lion's den	6
II.	The visions	7—12
	A. The four beasts	7
	B. The ram and the goat	8
	C. Daniel's prayer	9
	D. The angel's revelation	10—12

WHERE? The events described in the first section of Daniel occur in the court of Nebuchadnezzar. The prophetic section reflects the events of the several empires in the ancient Near East.

WHEN? Traditional and more conservative scholarship accept that the book of Daniel was written during the Babylonian captivity in the sixth century B.C.E. It is more likely that Daniel was written between 167 and 164 B.C.E., when the Jews were suffering persecution by the Syrian ruler Antiochus IV Epiphanes. If the later date is accepted, then Daniel is commentary on past and current events.

WHY? The book of Daniel is pastoral as well as prophetic, and offers hope and consolation to persecuted and suffering Jews.

HISTORICAL NARRATIVE

First and second Chronicles follow logically 1 and 2 Kings in that the same material is covered, although from a different perspective. Ezra and Nehemiah, which trace the postexilic history of the fifth century, are appropriately placed following the Chronicles. The original Hebrew Bible, however, places Ezra and Nehemiah before the Chronicles, and we will follow the ancient Hebrew order. All four books may be the work of a single author.

Ezra

Ezra describes the trying circumstances of postexilic life in Judah, at that time a small section of the Persian Empire.

WHO? Ezra, a priest and scribe, is the central figure in the story. Others include the following:

Artaxerxes	Persian emperor	4:7
Cyrus	Persian emperor	1:2
Darius	Persian emperor	6
Zerubbabel	Jewish leader	3:2

WHAT? Ezra is the account of reorganizing the restored Jewish community according to the principles of the Mosaic Torah. For protection against assimilation, Ezra forbids intermarriage between the Jews and foreigners. Ezra is structured as follows:

I. Restoration of the community	1—6
II. Ezra's particular mission	7—10
A. Ezra introduced and commissioned	7
B. Ezra's return to Jerusalem	8
C. The purity of God's people	9—10

WHERE? The recorded events take place in Babylonia and Judah.

WHEN? There is some disagreement among scholars about the precise date of Ezra's activities, but it was likely during the second term of the reign of Artaxerxes (ca. 425 B.C.E.). (See Appendix B, fig. 4.)

WHY? Ezra recounts the return of the Jewish people to Jerusalem and forbids intermarriage to prevent assimilation with the Gentile population.

Nehemiah

Nehemiah is the account of the rebuilding and reorganization of Judah after the exile.

WHO? Nehemiah, the Persian-appointed governor of Judah, has the primary responsibility for the rebuilding. Ezra also has a prominent place in the story. Those resisting Nehemiah's efforts include the following:

Sanballat	governor of Samaria
Tobiah	an Amorite
Geshem	an Arab

WHAT? Linked to Ezra, the book of Nehemiah continues the account of the resettlement of Jerusalem and expands our understanding of the conditions at that time in Judah. Nehemiah, concerned about these difficult conditions, is commissioned by Artaxerxes to return to Jerusalem to undertake the restoration. He rebuilds the wall around the city to provide defense and institutes social order. Ezra reintroduces Mosaic law, and a Jewish religious life is restored. The book may be outlined as follows:

I.	Nehemiah's commission and governorship	1—7
II.	Religious observances restored	8—10
III.	Organization of the Jewish community	11—13

WHERE? The events recorded occur in Jerusalem and the surrounding region of Judah.

WHEN? If Nehemiah was commissioned by Artaxerxes I, then the events took place between 445 and 433 B.C.E.

WHY? Nehemiah, as does Ezra, records the restoration of Judah and Jerusalem and stresses religious exclusivism in order to preserve the national and religious identity of the Jewish people.

1 and 2 Chronicles

The story of David and his royal descendants is retold from the point of view of the priestly class in 1 and 2 Chronicles. David is described more in terms of religious issues than military conquests, and little is said about David's flaws. The other kings are also discussed in reference to their loyalty to the Temple worship.

WHO? David, his contemporaries, and his successors (most of whom we have met) are the main characters in the Chronicles.

WHAT? The focus is on the place of David as founder of the worship in the Jerusalem Temple and Solomon as the builder of the Temple. Later kings are discussed in terms of their interest in the Temple. There is an account of the "true Israel." The books, taken together as the work of a single historian, may be outlined as follows:

I.	Genealogies from Adam to Saul	1 Chr. 1—9
II.	The reign of David	1 Chr. 10—29

III. The reign of Solomon   2 Chr. 1—9
IV. The Davidic monarchy to the exile   2 Chr. 10—36

WHERE? The events recorded take place in ancient Israel.

WHEN? The events span the history of the Davidic monarchy. The books were most likely written in the late fifth century B.C.E.

WHY? The clear intent of the writer is to trace the story of the true Israel, the one that faithfully worships Yahweh, and to point out how later kings who were unfaithful caused the collapse of the monarchy and the nation's downfall.

BETWEEN THE TESTAMENTS

The Old Testament narrative ends with King Cyrus's proclamation of liberty for the exiles, their return, and the restoration of Jewish life in Judah. There is a gap of several hundred years before the New Testament was composed. During this intertestamental period, the Jewish people experienced dramatic events, and a number of religious books shed light on this period. Some religious traditions have given these books near-canonical status. It is beyond the scope of our brief account to review this history and literature. But it may help to list the books known as the Apocrypha, regarded by the Roman Catholic and Greek Orthodox churches as deuterocanonical (second canon). The Apocrypha includes the following books:

1 and 2 Esdras   Ecclesiasticus
Tobit   Baruch
Judith   Additions to Daniel
Additions to Esther   1 and 2 Maccabees
The Wisdom of Solomon

Other writings about this period, called the Pseudepigrapha, were not admitted to the canon of either the Hebrew or Greek editions of the Bible. But both the Pseudepigrapha and the Apocrypha are important because they give us a view of the theological trends and religious practices of later Judaism, thus providing a crucial link between the Old and New Testaments. It is to the New Testament that we now turn.

PART THREE

THE NEW TESTAMENT

6

The Gospels

The New Testament is made up of twenty-seven pieces of literature, which may be classified in a variety of ways. For our purposes, we will divide these early Christian documents into three groups: the Gospels, the writings that trace the historical development of the early Christian community (Acts and the Pauline epistles), and the general epistles and Revelation.

The Gospels address the life and work of Jesus of Nazareth, not from the perspective of a modern-day historian but from the perspective of the "good news." The writers of these four accounts include extended sermons, proclaiming the saving power of the life and consummate death and resurrection of Jesus. Because the Gospels are not biographies, but *evangelion* (good news), they leave us with questions about our access to the "historical Jesus."[1] The theological orientation of the Gospel writers give us "the Christ of faith," and we are left to wonder about the correlation between the historical Jesus and the Christ who is the object of faith.

The Gospel authors use many images to characterize the Christ of faith. For example, they speak of him as the long-awaited Messiah, and Jesus becomes known as the Christ (*Christos*), a Greek translation of *messiah* (Mk. 14:62). He is called "Son of God" (Mk. 1:11), and Jesus frequently chooses "Son of Man" to refer to himself (Mt. 8:20). All these titles point in some way to the divine character of Jesus.

The first three Gospels share a common point of view, and therefore are frequently called the Synoptics. A careful reading suggests some interdependence, and the tracing of this linkage is called the Synoptic Problem. Many scholars place Mark as the earliest of the three Synoptic Gospels, with Matthew and Luke drawing upon Mark for their writing. It is likely that Matthew and Luke also had additional sources, called Q (*Quelle*, German for source), that were common to both. In addition, Matthew and Luke had sources that were used exclusively by each. It is possible to trace the development of the Gospels in six stages:[2]

1. The oral stage, during which the sayings and tradition were preserved (ca. 35–50 C.E.)
2. The Q stage, during which an anonymous scribe collected many sayings of Jesus (ca. 50–60 C.E.)
3. The Gospel of Mark (ca. 66–70 C.E.)
4. The Gospel of Matthew, drawing upon Mark, Q, and other sources (ca. 85 C.E.)
5. The Gospel of Luke, drawing upon Mark, Q, and other sources (ca. 90 C.E.)
6. The Gospel of John (ca. 100 C.E.)

Let us turn first to Mark, given its relatively early date.

The Gospel of Mark

The Gospel of Mark portrays Jesus as the Son of God (1:1), who proclaims the kingdom of God (1:15) and suffers death in obedience to God (8:31).

WHO? Mark fills his story of Jesus with interesting people and groups:

Barabbas	convicted terrorist	15:7f.
Bartimaeus	blind man	10:46f.
Caiaphas	high priest	14:63
Herod Antipas	ruler of Galilee	6:17–29
John the Baptist	prophet	1:4–9, 6:17
Joseph of Arimathea	ruling elder	15:43
Judas	disloyal disciple	14:10–11
Mary of Magdala	follower of Jesus	15:40
Peter	disciple	14:26ff.
Pharisees	group of law-observant Jews	14:53ff.
Pontius Pilate	Roman procurator	15:1ff.
Sadducees	group of devout Jews	14:53ff.
Sanhedrin	Jewish governing council	14:53–65
Scribes	experts in Mosaic law	12:28–34
Simon of Cyrene	man who carried cross of Jesus	15:21

WHAT? Mark's account is motivated by his conclusion that the death and resurrection of Jesus Christ are the fulfillment of the intention of God. The first half of the Gospel describes Jesus' ministry in Galilee (chapters 1–7), and the second half recounts the trip to and concluding events in Jerusalem (chapters 8–16). The Gospel may be outlined as follows:

I.	The mission of Jesus	1:1–3:6
	A. Preparation for the mission	1:1–13
	B. The mission proclaimed and demonstrated	1:14–45
	C. The ensuing conflict	1:46–3:6

II.   The Galilean mission   3:7–8:30
      A. Jesus calls followers   3:7–35
      B. Jesus teaches in parables   4:1–34
      C. Jesus performs miracles   4:35–5:43
      D. Conflict within   6:1–6
      E. The mission of the twelve   6:7–13
      F. The death of John the Baptist   6:14–29
      G. More miracles   6:30–8:10
      H. Misunderstanding   8:11–30
III. The mission revealed   8:30–10:52
      A. The predictions of death   8:31–10:45
      B. Blind eyes opened   10:46–52
IV.   The mission culminated in Jerusalem   11:1–16:8
      A. Teaching in the Temple   11:1–12:44
      B. Anticipatory teaching   13:1–37
      C. The final days   14:1–42
      D. The trial and death of Jesus   14:43–15:47
      E. The empty tomb   16:1–8
      F. A disputed longer ending that may have
          been added later   16:9–20

WHERE? The events recorded in Mark occur in Galilee and Judea. Among the places to note are the following:

Bethany   11:15–19
Capernaum   1:21–32
Gethsemane (just outside Jerusalem)   14:32–52
Jericho   10:46–52
Jerusalem   11:1ff.
Jordan River   1:9–11
Sea of Galilee   4:35–5:43
Nazareth   6:1–6
(See Appendix B, fig. 8.)

WHEN? The events of Jesus' life, recorded by Mark, take place between 25 and 35 C.E. The Gospel of Mark was most likely written between 65 and 70 C.E.

WHY? Mark's proclamation of the "good news" is not an upbeat portrayal of the life, mission, and passion of Jesus. Mark depicts Jesus as a misunderstood and suffering Messiah who ultimately triumphs over death, a triumph that brings hope to all who believe.

The Gospel of Matthew

Most scholars believe Matthew was written later than Mark and is dependent upon Mark. Matthew, however, edits Mark and adds several sections not found in Mark. These sections underline Matthew's conviction that Jesus is Israel's expected Messiah, and the disciples of Jesus are called to a life of obedience and righteousness.

WHO? Many of the characters and groups introduced in Mark reappear in Matthew. Other characters whom Matthew introduces include the following:

Disciples	original band of Jesus' followers	4:18–22
Herod the Great	ruler in Palestine	2:1–23
Jesus' ancestors	genealogy	1:1–10
Joseph	father of Jesus	1:8–25
The magi	wise men from the East	2:1–23
Mary	the mother of Jesus	1:8–25
Matthew	disciple, tax collector	9:9–13

WHAT? Matthew's Gospel is well-structured and has the following form:

I.	Jesus introduced as Messiah		1:1–4:16
	A.	Jesus meets long-held expectations	1:1–25
	B.	The birth of Jesus	2:1–23
	C.	Jesus' preparation for the messianic mission	3:1–4:16
II.	The ministry and teaching of Jesus the Messiah		4:17–16:20
	A.	Jesus calls disciples	4:17–22
	B.	Jesus' teaching	4:23–7:29
	C.	Jesus' ministry	8:1–9:34
	D.	The commissioning of the twelve	9:35–11:1
	E.	Jesus faces opposition	11:2–12:50
	F.	Jesus teaches in parables	13:1–52
	G.	More opposition and the death of John the Baptist	13:53–14:12
	H.	The continuing ministry	14:13–16:12
	I.	The disciples' confession	16:13–20
III.	Jesus culminates his mission in Jerusalem		16:21–28:20
	A.	The journey to Jerusalem and Jesus' prediction of his death	16:21–21:11
	B.	The Temple conversations	21:12–23:39
	C.	Treatise on the end times	24:1–25:46
	D.	The trial and crucifixion	26:1–27:66
	E.	The resurrection	28:1–20

Matthew, in his portrayal of Jesus, includes five major discourses. They are as follows:

1.	The Sermon on the Mount	5—7
2.	Commissioning of the twelve	10
3.	Parables of the kingdom	13
4.	Instructions to the church	18
5.	Warnings about the end times	23—25

Several well-known passages in Matthew include the following:

The Beatitudes	5:3–11
The Lord's Prayer	6:9–13
The Golden Rule	7:12
The Great Commandment	22:36–40
The Great Commission	28:18–20

WHERE? The events recorded in Matthew's Gospel took place in Galilee, Judea, and Egypt. The climax of Matthew's story, of course, occurred in Jerusalem.

WHEN? It is not easy to peg the exact date of Jesus' birth, but most scholars place it between 6 and 4 B.C.E. If Jesus' public life began about his thirtieth year and lasted from two to three years, then Jesus' death would have occurred prior to 30 C.E. Matthew's Gospel was probably written about 85 C.E.

WHY? Like the other Gospel writers, Matthew is not a biographer of the life of Jesus, but one who proclaims the good news. The good news of Matthew is that Jesus is the long-awaited Messiah, who follows the path of higher righteousness and expects his disciples to do the same. God is present to those who take this bold step of radical discipleship, living as true subjects of the kingdom of heaven.

The Gospel of Luke

Luke's Gospel is the first volume of a two-volume work (Luke-Acts). Luke portrays the story of Jesus as an integral part of God's plan of salvation for all of humanity and then describes the work of God through the church in the book of Acts. The emphasis in Luke is not on the immediacy of Christ's return as the culmination of God's work in world history, but on the historical development and mission of the church as the instrument of God's purposes in history. Luke contains much material that is unique to this Gospel, including the teaching purported to have been given to his disciples on the journey to Jerusalem (9:51–18:14). Otherwise, Luke essentially follows the chronology of Mark.

WHO? Jesus, of course, is the central figure in Luke's Gospel. Many believe the author was the physician Luke who accompanied Paul on some of the missionary journeys. Other scholars, given the date and composition of the Gospel, question that. The author was a polished writer and probably a Gentile as evidenced by the character of the writing and the mastery of the Greek language. Other characters in the story include the following:

Ancestors of Jesus	another genealogy	3:23–38
Anna	prophetess	2:36–38
Cleopas	one who met Jesus on Emmaus road	24:13–35
Elizabeth	mother of John the Baptist	1:5–20
Good Samaritan	character in a story told by Jesus	10:25–36
Lazarus	poor man in a story told by Jesus	16:19–31
Martha	sister of Mary	10:38–42
Mary	sister of Martha	10:38–42
Prodigal Son	character in a parable told by Jesus	15:11–32
Rich young ruler	man who asked Jesus about eternal life	18:18–26
Simeon	devout Jew	2:22–35
Simon	devout Jew	4:38–41
Theophilus	one to whom this Gospel is sent	1:1–4
Zacchaeus	tax collector who meets Jesus	19:1–10
Zechariah	priest and father of John the Baptist	1:5–79

WHAT? Luke's narrative of Jesus has a clearly stated purpose: "after investigating everything carefully from the very first, to write an orderly account for you, most excellent Theophilus, so that you may know the truth concerning the things about which you have been instructed" (1:3–4). Luke's "orderly account" has the following structure:

I.	Dedication to Theophilus	1:1–4
II.	The birth and infancy of Jesus	1:5–2:52
III.	The preparation for Jesus' mission	3:1–4:13
	A. The role of John the Baptist	3:1–22
	B. The ancestors of Jesus	3:23–38
	C. The temptations of Jesus	4:1–13
IV.	The ministry of Jesus in Galilee	4:14–9:50

V.	The trip to Jerusalem	9:51–19:44
VI.	The events in Jerusalem	19:45–21:38
VII.	The final days and death of Jesus	22:1–23:56
VIII.	The resurrection narrative	24:1–53

Some material in Luke is distinctive. For example, there are the accounts of:

The boy Jesus in the Temple	2:41–52
The raising of the widow's son at Nain	7:11–17
The dialogue with Mary and Martha	10:38–42
Jesus' visit with Zacchaeus	19:1–10

In addition, Luke records several of the well-known parables of Jesus:

The Good Samaritan	10:29–37
The Prodigal Son	15:11–32
The rich man and Lazarus	16:19–31
The Pharisee and the tax collector	18:9–14

WHERE? The events recorded by Luke take place in Galilee and Judea.

WHEN? It is widely accepted that Jesus lived during the first thirty years of the first century, although his birth may have preceded the turn of the century. Luke is variously dated by scholars, but it was probably written near 90 C.E.

WHY? The writer of Luke may have thought of world history as made up of three periods: the time of Israel, the time of Jesus, and the time of the church. He picks up the story, describing the time of Jesus, and then moves to an account of the church in the book of Acts. The cohering theme in both books is that God is working out the divine plan in world history. Jesus is at the center of this plan, linking Israel's past to the future age of the universal church.

The Gospel of John

The Gospel of John is quite different from the Synoptic Gospels. John portrays Jesus, not as an apocalyptic healer-exorcist, but as the embodiment of heavenly wisdom. Jesus is the Redeemer, sent from God to reveal God's will and glory on earth as the divine Word (*logos*, 1:1). While John records Jesus' healing events and other miracles, his writing is more of a meditation on the theological significance of Jesus' life and death. Whereas the Synoptics point to a second coming (the Parousia), John emphasizes the eternal presence of God in the form of the Paraclete or Holy Spirit.

WHO? Central to John's theological interpretation is the earthly figure of Jesus and his disciples. John introduces us to these disciples and others, including the following:

Andrew	disciple of Jesus and brother of Peter	1:35–42
Annas	father-in-law of high priest	18:12–14
James	son of Zebedee and brother of John	21:2
John	son of Zebedee and brother of James	21:2
Lazarus	brother of Mary and Martha	11:38–44
Nathanael	disciple of Jesus	1:43–51
Nicodemus	leader among the Jews	3:1–10
Philip	disciple of Jesus	1:43–51
Thomas	disciple of Jesus	20:24–29
Woman of Samaria	she questioned Jesus at Jacob's well	4:1–42

WHAT? John is more concerned with theological reflection than about the chronology of Jesus' public ministry. The book tends to be organized around themes, although a rough chronology is present. The material is organized as follows:

I.	Beginnings	1:1–51
	A. Theological prologue	1:1–18
	B. Preparation for the mission	1:19–51
II.	Signs and miracles revealing God's will and glory	2:1–11:57
III.	The passion of Jesus as the manifestation of God's glory	12:1–20:31
IV.	The epilogue	21:1–25

A distinctive feature of this book is the seven miraculous deeds, spaced to develop the theme of the Gospel, which is the revelation of Christ's divine nature:

1.	Changing water into wine	2:1–11
2.	Healing the nobleman's son	4:46–54
3.	Healing the impotent man	5:1–9
4.	Feeding the five thousand	6:1–14
5.	Walking on the water	6:16–21
6.	Healing the blind man	9:1–12
7.	Raising Lazarus	11:1–46

In addition, there are the "I am" statements of Jesus:

the bread of life	6:35
the light of the world	8:12; 9:5

the door	10:7
the good shepherd	10:11, 14
the resurrection and the life	11:25
the way, the truth, and the life	14:6
the true vine	15:1

WHERE? The events recorded by John take place in Galilee and Judea. There is also mention of Samaria, a region north of Judea (4:1–42).

WHEN? John reflects on the life and mission of Jesus. It is not easy to say precisely when the Gospel was written or by whom, but most scholars propose a date of approximately 100 C.E.

WHY? The author of the Gospel of John states his reason for writing: "Now Jesus did many other signs in the presence of his disciples, which are not written in this book. But these are written so that you may come to believe that Jesus is the Messiah, the Son of God, and that through believing you may have life in his name" (20:31). The author of John's Gospel writes to persuade readers to believe (a verb that occurs ninety-eight times in the Gospel), so that in believing, the reader may find and lead a true and obedient life.

7

The Early Christian Community: Acts and the Pauline Epistles

A substantial body of literature was written to guide the early Christian community. The literature, richly varied and nuanced, is historical, theological, and practical. The most prolific writers of this literature were Luke and Paul, and we turn first to Luke's account of the development of the early church in the book of Acts.

Acts

The Gospel of Luke and the Acts of the Apostles are two volumes of a single work. The first volume deals with the life, death, and resurrection of Jesus. The second volume provides a selective account of the growth of a universal faith intended for all nations.

WHO? The author recounts a remarkable story of the early church, with the apostle Peter as the dominant character in the first half of Acts and the apostle Paul as the main character in the second half. Others in the story include the following:

Apollos	Christian worker	18:24–28
Antonius Felix	Roman governor	24
Barnabas	Jewish Christian worker	11—14
Cornelius	Roman centurion	10
Gallio	Roman Proconsul	18:12–17
Gamaliel	Jewish teacher	5:34
Herod Agrippa	ruler in Judea and Samaria	12:1–19
James	Jesus' kinsman	15:13
Philip	early disciple	8:11–40
Porcius Festus	Roman governor	25
Simon	magician	8:9–13
Stephen	disciple	6—8

WHAT? The author of Acts divides his account of the early church into the sections revolving around the ministries of Peter and Paul. The first half (chapters 1—12) is an account of Jewish Christianity and the Jerusalem church, culminating with Peter's conversion to a wider perspective on the mission of church (10—11). The second half is devoted to Paul's mission work to the Gentiles in the Greco-Roman world. The book is structured as follows:

I.	Prologue	1:1–3
II.	The beginning of the church	1:4–12:25
	A. Its formation in Jerusalem	1:4–2:47
	B. Its difficulties	3:1–7:60
	C. Its expansion	8:1–12:25
III.	The ministry of Paul	13:1–28:31
	A. The first missionary tour	13:1–14:28
	B. The council of Jerusalem	15:1–35
	C. The second missionary tour	15:36–18:28
	D. The third missionary tour	19:1–21:14
	E. Paul the prisoner	21:15–28:31

WHERE? The growth of the early church, according to the author, begins in Jerusalem, expands to Judea and Samaria, and then with the journeys of Paul, expands to the "ends of the earth" (the far reaches of the Roman Empire). Places to note are as follows:

Antioch	11; 18
Areopagus (a hill in Athens)	17:19
Athens	17:16–18:17
Caesarea	24
Corinth	18:1–17
Cyprus	13:4
Ephesus	19
Galatia	16:6
Iconium	14:1–7
Jerusalem	15:1–35; 21:1–23:35
Judea/Judah	1:8; 2:14
Lystra	14:8
Macedonia	16:8–10
Malta (also called Melita)	28:1
Philippi	16:11–40
Rome	28:11–31
Samaria	8:4–25
Thessalonica	17:1–9
Troas	20:5–12

WHEN? The author of Acts, who was possibly Luke, the companion of Paul, most likely wrote Luke-Acts between 80 and 85 C.E. The period covered in the account is from approximately 30 to 60 C.E.; Paul was imprisoned in Rome and executed there in about 62 C.E.

WHY? Luke-Acts is not modern critical history, but for its time, it is reputable history. The author, however, is concerned about more than describing events; he attempts to discern the underlying meaning of the events. Acts, coupled with Luke, unfolds the pattern of the divine purpose of establishing a new community of justice and universal inclusivism, embodying the teaching of Jesus. The message is carried across the Roman Empire with the endorsement of the apostles and especially Peter, the first leader of the emergent church. Careful to articulate the relationship of Christianity to Judaism, the author describes Christianity's movement into the wider world of the Gentiles. (See Appendix B, fig. 9.)

THE LETTERS OF PAUL

It is hard to overstate the importance of Paul in the development of the early Christian community. The former Pharisee and persecutor of the Christian church led the mission to the Gentiles and wrote several of the books of the New Testament. Traditionally, he was considered to be the author of thirteen or fourteen of the twenty-seven books of the New Testament, but literary historians now attribute seven and perhaps one or two more to him.

Paul's letters have greatly influenced the reading of the New Testament and the development of later Christianity. Of particular significance is Paul's interpretation of the meaning of Jesus' death and its importance for human salvation. Paul asserts that the crucifixion (and resurrection) introduce a fundamentally different relationship between God and all humanity. Faith in Christ, Paul maintains, supersedes Torah obedience, and redemption for the whole human family comes by grace through faith in Jesus Christ.

Some have argued that there is almost more of Paul than Jesus in classical Christianity, and it is true that Paul does not emphasize Jesus' teaching about the kingdom of God. But a case can be made that Paul's mystical emphasis on spiritual union with the divine is not unlike God's reign in human life.

There are a few historical inconsistencies in the account of Paul's ministry in the book of Acts and of the unfolding of his ministry in the letters. As a general rule, the references in Paul's letters are closer to the events of his missionary journeys than the account in Acts and are therefore more reliable accounts.

Paul's use of letters follows the accepted form of correspondence in his time, diverging only to accommodate his Christian message and the particular situations in the churches to which he writes. His letters were so effective and so widely circulated that others used this approach and may have borrowed his name. It is safe to attribute Romans, 1 and 2 Corinthians, Galatians, Philippians, 1 Thessalonians, and Philemon to Paul. Colossians may also be authentically Pauline. There is doubt about 2 Thessalonians and Ephesians, and Titus and 1 and 2 Timothy are later works by one of Paul's disciples.

The early letters of Paul, and indeed nearly all the writing of Paul, have an eschatological theme. There is new life in Christ, and we now await Christ's return. First Thessalonians epitomizes these themes.

1 Thessalonians

The oldest book in the New Testament, 1 Thessalonians, was written about 50 C.E. from Corinth to the church at Thessalonica, the capital city of Macedonia. Paul and his companions, Timothy and Silas, had founded the church, but Paul was forced to flee (Acts 7:7) and so he is naturally concerned about the conditions in the church.

WHO? Paul, with his colleagues Timothy and Silas (Silvanus), address this letter to the young Christians at Thessalonica. Paul and his companions base their remarks to the church in Thessalonica on a first-hand report from Timothy (3:6–10).

WHAT? Paul has a fairly long introductory section in which he attempts to nurture the new Christians in the Thessalonian church. Most of these Christians were Greek converts from polytheistic religions. He then moves to his primary reason for writing, which is to help these Christians hold fast to their new faith, even though the end time is fast approaching. The letter may be outlined as follows:

I.	Salutation	1:1
II.	On remaining faithful	1:2–3:13
	A. Gratitude for the faithfulness of the Thessalonians	1:2–10
	B. Exhortation to continue to live faithfully	2:1–3:13
III.	Practical guidance in reference to the coming of the Lord	4:1–5:24
	A. Living a life pleasing to God	4:1–12
	B. Guidance about Christ's return	4:13–5:11
	C. Final thoughts and benediction	5:12–28

WHERE? Paul writes from the Greek seaport of Corinth to the church in Thessalonica, an important city in the Roman province of Macedonia and the center of Roman administration for the region. (See Appendix B, fig. 10.)

WHEN? The letter is written with assistance from Timothy and Silas in about 50 or 51 C.E.

WHY? The three missionaries, Paul, Timothy, and Silas, wrote the letter because some of the Thessalonian Christians were convinced that they would live to see the second coming. Guidance about the Parousia is given, as well as a caution about undue speculation regarding the end times. In addition, Paul and his companions urge the Thessalonian Christians to live godly lives in the present, even though the second coming could soon occur.

1 Corinthians

In writing to the Corinthians, Paul is concerned about "unity in the Spirit." He urges them to abandon their divisive behavior and to work together for their mutual benefit and common good. He addresses some critical issues that have led to factionalism and conflict.

WHO? In addition to the author, Paul, the letter introduces the reader to:

Apollos	a Christian Jew from Alexandria	1:12
Cephas	the apostle Peter	1:12

WHAT? To overcome the conflict in the congregation, Paul attempts to guide the Corinthians concerning critical issues such as different kinds of wisdom (1:10–3:23), Christian ethics and responsibility (5:1–11:1), communion behavior (11:17–34), the gifts of the Spirit (chapters 12—14), and the resurrection of the dead (chapter 15).

The letter has the following structure:

I.	Salutation and thanksgiving	1:1–9
II.	Conflict in the church	1:10–4:21
III.	Critical problems for Christians, including sexual ethics and legal action	5:1–6:20
IV.	Replies to questions	7:1–16:4
	A. Celibacy and marriage	7:1–40
	B. Freedom and food offered to idols	8:1–11:1
	C. Public worship and spiritual gifts	11:2–14:40
	D. The resurrection of the dead	15:1–55
	E. The collection for the saints	16:1–4
V.	Information and greetings	16:5–24

Of special note is Paul's magnificent hymn of love in chapter 13.

WHERE? Paul probably wrote to the Corinthians from Ephesus. He demonstrates a good understanding of the cultures and circumstances of Corinth, a wealthy port city noted for its pagan rituals and sexual vices and the cult of the love goddess Aphrodite (Venus).

WHEN? Most scholars date the Corinthian correspondence around 52 to 54 C.E., after 1 Thessalonians and prior to Romans.

WHY? Paul wrote to the Corinthians because he had received troubling reports about the church he was instrumental in founding. He wanted to get the congregation back on course, for it was conflicted and morally lax. He argues that they belong to one another, should live in the unity of the Spirit, and should follow the way of Christ.

2 Corinthians

A composite letter, 2 Corinthians is possibly the product of several sittings or the combinations of fragments. It is a letter of strong passion in which Paul asserts his apostolic authority while at the same time reflecting his strong bond with the Corinthian Christians.

WHO? In addition to Paul and the Corinthian Christians, the reader is introduced to one of Paul's companions and coworkers, Titus (7:6; 8:16).

WHAT? As a compendium of several letters or fragments of letters, 2 Corinthians contains comments and reflections on quite different situations, often expressed in contrasting tones. For example, the harsh tone of chapters 10—13 contrasts with the conciliatory tone of chapters 1—9. There are six major sections of the letters:

I.	The introduction	1:1–11
II.	Paul's postponement of a visit and assurance of concern	1:12–2:13
III.	Paul's mission and ministry	2:14–7:4
IV.	Paul's future plans for the church	7:5–9:15
V.	Paul's defense of his apostolic authority	10:1–13:10
VI.	Admonitions, greetings, and benedictions	13:11–13

WHERE? Assuming the composite character of 2 Corinthians, it is possible to posit at least two occasions and locations for composition. Chapters 1—9 were probably sent from Macedonia (perhaps Philippi) after some encouraging news, and chapters 10—13 sent later, also from Macedonia, after Paul received some alarming news.

WHEN? The first major section of 2 Corinthians was written about 55 C.E., the next section about one year later.

WHY? Second Corinthians was written because the relationship between Paul and the Corinthian church had deteriorated. The relationship was jeopardized because of other missionaries working in Corinth who may have been "Judaizers" who questioned Paul's apostolic status. Paul, displaying his own human weaknesses, boldly asserts his authority and calls on the Corinthians to live faithfully. He argues that human relationship with God is on a new basis. "So if anyone is in Christ, there is a new creation: everything old has passed away; see, everything has become new!" (2 Cor. 5:17).

Galatians

Although the origin of this letter is not known for sure, it is generally agreed that the letter was written by Paul. The letter reflects his ongoing struggle to defend his apostolic authority, as in the Corinthian correspondence. But it is more than a strong declaration of his right to preach a Christianity independent from Judaism; it is also a vigorous statement of the gospel, that faith in Christ is the path to divine acceptance, not obedience to Torah commandments.

WHO? The letter reflects Paul's strong feelings about the way the "foolish Galatians" (3:1) are being led astray by "Judaizers." To make his case, Paul mentions several others whom we have met:

Abraham	patriarch	3:6–18
Barnabus	Paul's coworker	2:13
Cephas (Peter)	apostle	1:8; 2:11
Hagar	servant in Abraham's household	4:24–25
James	kinsman of Jesus	1:19
Sarah	wife of Abraham	4:26
Titus	Paul's coworker	2:1

WHAT? Paul's argument is powerful and direct. He asserts that he is a true apostle, equal in authority to those in Jerusalem, and the gospel of justification by faith in Christ replaces the works of the law. His argument has five components:

I.	Defense of his apostleship	1:1–2:14
II.	His essential gospel: justification by faith	2:15–3:29
III.	Christians are true children of God	4:1–31
IV.	Christians are free from Mosaic law	5:1–6:10
V.	Concluding summary and benediction	6:11–18

WHERE? Paul probably writes from Ephesus to Christians in the Roman province of Galatia, which included the cities of Iconium, Lystra, and Derbe. However, some have suggested that an area in north central Asia Minor (modern-day Turkey), which was also called Galatia and where Paul had traveled and preached, might have been the destination of the letter (Acts 16:6). (See Appendix B, fig. 10.)

WHEN? The date of Paul's writing is also disputed, but most scholars believe the letter was written in about 55 C.E.

WHY? The occasion for the writing is clear, to counter those who insisted that the Galatian Christians observe Jewish laws and customs, especially the practice of circumcision. Paul defends the Gentile's freedom as integral to the gospel of justification by faith. He writes: "For freedom Christ has set us free" (5:1a). He also writes: "There is no longer Jew or Greek, there is no longer slave or free, there is no longer male and female; for all of you are one in Christ Jesus" (3:28).

Romans

In Romans, we have Paul's most comprehensive statement of his understanding of the gospel and his most influential letter. It is his longest letter and the most carefully constructed and argued. Unlike his other letters, Paul addresses this letter to a church that he had not founded or even visited.

WHO? Paul uses several Old Testament characters in the development of his case with the Roman Christians. He uses Adam (5:12–14), Abraham (4:1–5), and David (4:6–8) in his argument. In chapter 16, he sends personal greetings to several people, including Phoebe (16:1), who is commended to the Roman Christians.

WHAT? Paul uses his letter to the Romans to develop his understanding of the Christian faith in a systematic way. At the heart of his understanding is his belief that humankind stands in need of redemption, a redemption that comes through faith in God's gracious activity in Jesus Christ. The argument unfolds in ten major sections:

I.	Salutation and prayer of thanksgiving	1:1–15
II.	The statement of the theme	1:16–17
III.	The guilt of the human family	1:18–3:31
IV.	Abraham as the model of faith	4:1–25
V.	Justification through Christ and deliverance from sin and death	5:1–7:25

VI.	Life in the Spirit	8:1–39
VII.	God's righteousness with Israel	9:1–11:36
VIII.	Behavior in the church and the world	12:1–15:13
IX.	Paul's reason for writing	15:14–33
X.	Appendix of greetings	16:1–27

WHERE? Paul most likely wrote the letter to the Christians in Rome from Corinth.

WHEN? Most scholars date the composition about 55 to 56 C.E.

WHY? Paul writes in reference to the specific circumstances in the Roman church and is concerned about his relationship to the church. There were disputes between Jewish and Gentile Christians, and perhaps the Christians in Rome harbored some anxiety about Paul's leadership. But Paul uses these particular circumstances to articulate his mature theology of God's love expressed in Jesus Christ.

Philippians

Another of Paul's "authentic" letters, Philippians, was written while Paul was in jail in either Ephesus or Rome. Paul had founded the church at Philippi, a city in Macedonia, in about 50 C.E., making it the first European church. Philippian Christians were generous in sending Paul support, and Paul responds in gratitude and affection.

WHO? In his letter to the Philippian Christians, Paul mentions Timothy (1:1; 2:19–22); Epaphroditus, a coworker (2:25); and two Philippian women, Euodia and Syntyche, who had a disagreement (4:2).

WHAT? The letter addresses practical concerns, but as usual with Paul, he used these concerns to expand on his understanding of the gospel. Of particular note is his use of the Christian hymn that describes Jesus as one who empties himself, taking the form of a slave, being born in human likeness (2:5–11). This kenosis (emptying) leads to Christ's exaltation. The letter may be outlined as follows:

I.	Salutation	1:1–2
II.	Paul's thanksgiving and prayer for the Philippians	1:3–11
III.	Paul's news about himself and instructions for the Philippians	1:12–3:1
IV.	Exhortation to depend on God's justification, not those who insist on circumcision	3:2–4:1

V.	Urging that coworkers live in harmony	4:2–3
VI.	General instruction	4:4–9
VII.	Gratitude for financial support	4:10–20
VIII.	Closing greetings	4:21–30

WHERE? Paul wrote either from Ephesus or Rome to the Christians in the Macedonian city of Philippi.

WHEN? He probably wrote from Ephesus in about 56 C.E., but if the letter was written from Rome during his imprisonment, it would make Philippians a later composition (about 61 to 62 C.E.).

WHY? In addition to expressing his gratitude for the Philippian support, Paul writes to keep these Christians from being led astray by the proponents of circumcision. Such a path would detract from the beauty of God's love in Jesus Christ.

Philemon

Paul wrote this short letter to plead with Philemon to receive Philemon's runaway slave, Onesimus, who had left with some money. Onesimus had since been converted, and Paul asks that he be received as a Christian brother.

WHO? There are the two main characters in the story: Onesimus, the slave who has become a Christian under Paul's influence (v. 10); and Philemon, a Christian brother (v. 1) whom Paul is urging to receive Onesimus. Paul also mentions Timothy (v. 1); two Christians in Philemon's house, Apphia and Archippus (v. 2); and coworkers, Epaphras, Mark, Aristarchus, Demas, and Luke (vv. 23–24).

WHAT? The personal story in the letter is touching, but it is hard for us to ignore the larger issue of slavery, which is very much present in the correspondence. Paul uniformly showed respect for the current social order, but many have wondered why he did not denounce slavery as inconsistent with Christian belief in God's inclusive love for the whole human family. The letter has the following structure:

I.	Salutation and greeting	1—3
II.	Thanksgiving and prayers for Philemon	4—7
III.	Paul's pleas for Onesimus	8—21
IV.	Final greetings and benediction	23—25

WHERE? The letter was probably written during Paul's captivity in Ephesus, or, as some argue, during his imprisonment in Rome. The precise location of Philemon's house is not mentioned, but it is probably in Colossae.

WHEN? If the letter was written by Paul in Ephesus, then its date of composition was about 56 C.E.

WHY? Paul specifically asks that Onesimus be received back by Philemon, and in so doing, argues that faith is germane to all human relationships.

THE DISPUTED LETTERS OF PAUL

2 Thessalonians

Not all scholars agree that Paul is the author of this letter, and therefore we place it among the "disputed" Pauline letters. Its major themes, however, have some similarity to 1 Thessalonians. The author encourages the Thessalonian Christians to be responsible and faithful, and then he assists them in understanding the Parousia.

WHO? The salutation attributes the letter to Paul, Silas (Silvanus), and Timothy. Those scholars who question this authorship point to factors such as the differences in the understanding of the Parousia. The author of 1 Thessalonians speaks of the Parousia as coming "like a thief in the night"; 2 Thessalonians tells of apocalyptic signs that point to its arrival (e.g., the coming of the lawless one). Some, arguing for the Pauline origin of the letter, maintain that Silas and Timothy could have had a major part in the writing, and that Paul's views of the end times have developed and been expanded in 2 Thessalonians to make a point, whereas in 1 Thessalonians his ideas were incomplete.

WHAT? The author's point is that the "day of the Lord" has not yet arrived (2:2), even though a letter purported to be from Paul says that it has. Believers should not cease working in anticipation of the immediate return of Christ, but should continue to support themselves (3:11–12). The letter unfolds as follows:

I.	Salutation and thanksgiving	1:1–4
II.	Judgment at Christ's coming	1:5–12
III.	Instructions on doctrine and duty	2:1–3:15
	A. Doctrine about the day of the Lord	2:1–12
	B. Duty to be undertaken	2:13–3:15
IV.	Benediction	3:16–18

WHERE? If the letter is Pauline in origin, then it probably originated in Corinth and was sent to Thessalonica near the time of the writing of 1 Thessalonians. If not Pauline in origin, then its place of composition is unknown.

WHEN? As one of the "disputed" Pauline letters, it is difficult to date. Some, of course, place it alongside 1 Thessalonians. Others place it in the context of a much later persecution of the church, as late as the end of the first century.

WHY? The author has at least four reasons for writing. He wanted to oppose an interpretation of the day of the Lord that made it seem so near that the Thessalonian Christians were neglecting their responsibilities. He wanted to oppose letting the idle live off those who were fulfilling their everyday responsibilities. He wanted to strengthen the previous teaching of Paul. And he wanted to warn them about a previous letter attributed to Paul that he thought to be false and harmful. In general, the author wants to restore order in a confused congregation and urge faithfulness in the call of God (1:11).

Colossians

Although this letter possibly could have been written by Paul, the contents suggest that it was written by a disciple of Paul. The immediate occasion for writing is the appearance in Colossae of Christian teachers announcing a "philosophy" (2:8) to which the author of Colossians takes exception. The author counters with the claim that in Jesus "all the fullness of God was pleased to dwell" (1:19).

WHO? The author, probably a disciple of Paul, writes to the Christians at Colossae. The author mentions several colleagues of Paul in his final greeting: Tychicus, Aristarchus, Mark, Justus, Epaphras, Luke (the beloved physician), Nympha, and Archippus (4:7–17).

WHAT? Unlike the other letters of Paul, which emphasize the work of Christ (crucifixion and resurrection), Colossians is more christological. Refuting the false philosophy that apparently had blended pagan and Jewish elements about "elemental spirits of the universe" (2:8) and angels (2:18), the author asserts the preeminence of Christ. Christ is preeminent because the power now expressed in him is the same power that created the universe. Christians are to "receive Christ Jesus the Lord" and continue to live their lives in him (2:6). The argument is structured as follows:

I. Salutation   1:1–2
II. Thanksgiving and prayer that the Colossians will
      be faithful to Christ   1:3–20
III. Paul's apostolic authority and ministry   1:21–2:5
IV. False teaching contrasted with the way of Christ   2:6–23
V. Instructions in the Christian life   3:1–4:6
VI. Concluding greetings and instruction   4:7–18

WHERE? The letter is addressed to the Christians at Colossae, a small town in the Roman province of Asia located about a hundred miles southeast of Ephesus. If written by Paul, it was probably composed during his imprisonment in Ephesus. If the letter was not written by Paul, then the origin of the letter is unknown.

WHEN? If Pauline in origin, the letter was composed about 56 C.E., but the letter was more likely written later, with estimates ranging from 65 to 90 C.E.

WHY? The letter was written to counter false teaching, perhaps a form of gnosticism. The author, using a philosophical approach, argues that Christian faith is rooted in Jesus of Nazareth, who is the ground of all true philosophy, and that union with him is the essence of true religion.

Ephesians

While many scholars maintain Pauline authorship for Colossians, fewer argue that Paul wrote Ephesians. But the letter is a tribute to Paul, written by a later disciple who adapts Pauline ideas to the concerns of the time and place.

WHO? The letter resembles Colossians in style and thought and differs from the undisputed letters of Paul in vocabulary, literary style, and content. The author addresses the letter to the "saints" in Ephesus, although there is little reference to the Ephesian church, and no reference to coworkers.

WHAT? The theme of this epistle is that the unity found in the cosmos through Christ (1—3) should be reflected in the unity of the church (4—6). The argument unfolds as follows:

I. Greetings and blessing   1:1–14
II. Prayer and thanksgiving   1:15–23
III. From death to life   2:1–10

IV.	All one in Christ	2:11–22
V.	Apostolic ministry	3:1–21
VI.	Unity in the body of Christ	4:1–16
VII.	Christian duties	4:17–6:9
VIII.	Christian armor	6:10–20
IX.	Closing	6:21–24

WHERE? The letter is addressed to Christians in Ephesus, a port city in western Asia Minor. The letter may not have been exclusively for the Ephesian Christians, but a more general letter attached to the Pauline collection. Where the letter was written is unknown.

WHEN? If it is a "cover letter" for the Pauline collection, then it may have been written between 90 and 100 C.E. Some identify the letter with the lost letter to Laodicea (Col. 4:16).

WHY? It is unclear why the letter was written since no concrete situation is mentioned as the occasion for writing. The emphasis on unity in the church suggests some disunity, but no particular circumstances are described. It appears that the letter is an epistle (a general letter) with a didactic and pastoral purpose for more than one Christian congregation.

THE PASTORAL LETTERS

The three letters addressed to Paul's mission coworkers are called the pastorals, and while they are attributed to Paul, these letters reflect conditions that existed after Paul's time. They also reflect a more organized church and a different style and vocabulary than we find in the undisputed letters of Paul.

1 Timothy

This letter takes up the issue of false doctrine based on "myths and endless genealogies that promote speculations rather than the divine training that is known by faith" (1:4). The author warns against this false teaching and urges behavior in keeping with order and discipline in the church.

WHO? The letter is written by an unknown disciple, known as the Pastor, and it is addressed to Timothy, Paul's younger coworker. However, if the letter is mid-second century, then "Timothy" becomes the symbol of appropriate leadership in the church.

WHAT? The letter addresses the erroneous doctrine circulating at the time and proposes an appropriate order for church life in a postapostolic age. It may be outlined as follows:

I.	Salutation	1:1–2
II.	Warning against false teachers	1:3–20
III.	Order in the church	2:1–3:13
IV.	Dealing with inappropriate belief and practice	3:14–4:16
V.	Providing pastoral care	5:1–6:2
VI.	Warning and exhortation	6:3–19
VII.	Personal instructions and benediction	6:20–21

WHERE? If the letter is not from the hand of Paul, then it is difficult to locate the place of origin and destination. If it is from Paul, then the letter was probably written from Rome.

WHEN? The letter was probably written sometime between 65 and 100 C.E., although some scholars place the pastorals as late as the mid-second century.

WHY? First Timothy, like 2 Timothy and Titus, addresses conditions in a postapostolic era. These letters argue against a religious orientation based upon speculative mythology and asceticism. In addition, the author shows concern for good church order and appropriate behavior for deacons, presbyters, and bishops.

2 Timothy

Of the three pastorals, this letter is closest in tone to the authentic Pauline letters. There appears to be a genuine relationship between the author and Timothy. This letter is similar in content to 1 Timothy, showing concern for false teaching and appropriate behavior and order.

WHO? The section ending the letter (4:6–22) has a Pauline tone, but nonetheless most scholars attribute the letter to the Pastor. The origin and destination of the letter are unknown.

WHAT? Second Timothy may be outlined as follows:

I.	Salutation	1:1–2
II.	Thanksgiving	1:3–7
III.	Exhortation to live as a true disciple of Christ	1:8–2:13
IV.	Resisting false teaching	2:14–3:9
V.	The charge to Timothy	3:10–4:5
VI.	Personal instructions, greetings, and benediction	4:6–22

WHERE AND WHEN? As with 1 Timothy, it is not possible to state with certainty the time, origin, and destination of the letter, although it shares the approximate date of 1 Timothy.

WHY? The letter was written to encourage "Timothy" to rekindle gifts and be a "good soldier of Jesus Christ" (2:3). He is urged to combat false teaching with the "sacred writings" (3:15) and to use scripture to equip Christians for good works.

Titus

Once again, the author (the Pastor) may be using a name, Titus, to mean a church leader. The two concerns of the letter are order and false teaching.

WHO? The author is most likely the Pastor, who wrote 1 and 2 Timothy. At the end of the letter there is a reference to Artemas, Tychicus, Zenas, and Apollos, evidently coworkers.

WHAT? This relatively short letter may be divided into eight sections:

I.	Salutation	1:1–4
II.	Concerning elders	1:5–9
III.	Warnings about false teachers	1:10–16
IV.	Christian responsibilities	2:1–10
V.	On salvation	2:11–15
VI.	More on Christian duties	3:1–7
VII.	Recommendations to Titus	3:8–11
VIII.	Final messages and benediction	3:12–15

WHERE AND WHEN? If this letter is Pauline, then it may have been written in Ephesus. But it is more likely that Titus was written in a postapostolic period. There is mention of Crete, but it is difficult to reconstruct the particular circumstances of this reference.

WHY? The pastorals share the common concern of false teaching and church order, and Titus gives guidance on these two concerns.

8

The General Epistles and Revelation

Paul's use of the letter to communicate with individual churches influenced later authors whose writings became part of the New Testament. In fact, 1 and 2 Timothy and Titus borrowed Paul's name in order to give their writing the authority of the apostle. The eight writings known as the general epistles are addressed not to specific congregations but directly to the larger Christian community.

Seven of these writings are often called the catholic epistles in that they were intended for the whole church. Hebrews, although containing an ending like a Pauline letter, really makes little pretense of being a letter at all. It is a theological treatise or an extended sermon. It is impossible to determine the author of these epistles. Each of them, with the exception of Hebrews, is attributed to a prominent leader in the original Jerusalem church. The practice of pseudonymous authorship was not uncommon in the time in which these letters were written.

Hebrews

The author of Hebrews is a polished stylist who draws heavily upon the Old Testament, but there are traces of Greek philosophy as well. He is probably writing to Jewish Christians who are familiar with the Old Testament, and he develops the theme that Jesus is both the kingly and priestly Messiah. In Christ, the purpose of God is revealed, and Christ serves as the heavenly high priest and mediator for humanity.

WHO? The author of Hebrews is not known, but some New Testament scholars suggest Apollos, the Jewish convert mentioned in Acts 18. An older tradition maintained that Paul wrote Hebrews, but this view was disputed even in the early church, and few contemporary scholars argue for Pauline authorship.

Christ is the central figure of Hebrews and is viewed as the supreme revelation of God. The author makes this case by referring to several Old Testament characters who were people of faith. The list includes these names:

Aaron	7:11–14
Abel	11:4

Abraham	7:1–3; 11:8–12
Cain	11:4
Enoch	11:5
Isaac	11:9
Jacob	11:9, 21
Joseph	11:22
Joshua	4:3–10
Levi	7:4–10
Melchizedek	7:1–8:13
Moses	3:1–6; 11:23–28
Noah	11:7
Sarah	11:11

WHAT? The author of Hebrews maintains that Christ is the preeminent revelation of God. He is superior to the angels and even Moses, and as the great high priest from the line of Melchizedek, his sacrifice on the cross is superior to sacrifices in the Temple. Therefore, Christians should place their faith in Christ and endure whatever challenges come along. The author puts forth a series of arguments to sustain his theme and generally follows them with an exhortation. The writing is structured as follows:

I.	God has spoken in Jesus Christ	1:1–4
II.	Jesus Christ is superior	1:5–4:13
	A. To the angels	1:5–2:18
	B. To Moses	3:1–4:2
	C. To Joshua	4:3–13
III.	Jesus is the great high priest	4:14–10:39
	A. In the order of Mechizedek	4:14–7:28
	B. In his priestly ministry	8:1–10:39
IV.	Therefore live by faith in Christ	11:1–13:19
V.	Concluding exhortations	13:20–25

WHERE? The letter may have originated in Rome, and it was most likely intended for wide circulation, especially among Jewish Christians.

WHEN? Hebrews is quoted in a noncanonical writing, 1 Clement (about 96 C.E.), which means it was circulating before the end of the first century. Some scholars date Hebrews before 70 C.E., the time of the destruction of the Temple in Jerusalem, because of the mention of Temple worship. But the argument is not totally persuasive in that the references to Temple worship are speculative rather than historical.

WHY? The traditional view that Hebrews is a "sermon" to Jewish Christians who were slipping away from their faith has some merit, but nothing in the text requires this view. Hebrews does assume familiarity with the Old Testament, but the author also draws upon Hellenistic thought in his argument that earthly events and human institutions are reflections of invisible heavenly realities. The fundamental argument, however, is clear —that Christ is the supreme revelation of God and the high priest who fulfilled the Jewish order of sacrifice. He becomes the one who expiates our sin and gives us full access to God.

James

James, along with Hebrews, is really more of an extended sermon than a letter. Its contents are strongly ethical in character and have some similarity to the Old Testament book of Proverbs.

WHO? The authorship of James was traditionally ascribed to "the Lord's brother" (Gal. 1:19), but several factors make this claim difficult to sustain. For example, the book makes no reference to Jesus of Nazareth, and the Greek may be too polished for James, whose formal education was probably somewhat limited. The writing likely occurred after the death of James (ca. 62 C.E.), since Paul's writings would not have been widely circulated prior to 62 C.E. Further, a work of James, the leader of the Jerusalem church, would not have been seriously questioned for inclusion in the New Testament canon, yet inclusion of this book was questioned.

WHAT? The author speaks directly about Christian moral behavior, especially about the themes of testing, wisdom, wealth, and generosity. The argument is clear that the keeping of the law is the way to demonstrate true faith, and the law is epitomized by love (2:8). The book may be outlined as follows:

I.	Introduction to the epistle	1:1
II.	The major themes of the epistle	1:2–27
	A. Trials, wisdom, and wealth	1:2–11
	B. Temptation, speech, and good deeds	1:12–27
III.	The law of love	2:1–26
	A. Show no partiality	2:1–13
	B. Faith without works is dead	2:14–26
IV.	Appropriate speech	3:1–12
V.	Appropriate behavior	3:13–4:12
	A. Wisdom	3:13–18
	B. Friendship with the world	4:1–10
	C. Judgment	4:11–12

| VI. | Temptations and wealth | 4:13–5:6 |
| VII. | Patience and prayer | 5:7–20 |

WHEN? If the letter was written by James, the leader of the Jerusalem church, then a date preceding 62 C.E. would be necessary. However, given the questions surrounding the authorship of this book, the book's date may be placed around 88 to 90 C.E.

WHERE? The origin of the letter is difficult to determine, although references to poverty and generosity may suggest that the epistle is addressed to Christian communities experiencing economic distress.

WHY? If there is a cohering theme to James, then it is that true faith is expressed in good works. Religion is practical more than it is creedal or ritualistic. Of particular interest is the author's discussion of faith and works (2:14–26), a possible argument against Paul's doctrine of salvation through faith. At the very least, this section attempts to correct a misunderstanding of the Pauline doctrine of justification by faith.

1 Peter

The book of 1 Peter, like James, is characterized by its practical and ethical content. It may have been a baptismal sermon (3:21), and it underlines both the blessings and risks of adopting a Christian way of life.

WHO? The work presents itself as the work of the apostle Peter, written from Rome during the reign of Nero. It is addressed to persecuted Christians in Asia Minor. Many present-day scholars argue for a later date, once again making it difficult to ascribe authorship.

WHAT? The letter builds a case for discipline in both morals and theology. The foundation of these important domains of Christian life is the work of Christ. The author makes his case as follows:

I.	Salutation	1:1–3
II.	The foundation of hope	1:4–13
III.	The call to Christian living	1:13–2:10
	A. Holiness	1:13–21
	B. Ethical living	1:22–2:4
	C. Christ as the foundation stone	2:5–10
IV.	Relationship responsibilities	2:10–3:22
	A. To all people	2:10–17
	B. To slaves	2:18–25
	C. To wives	3:1–6

D.	To husbands	3:7
E.	In general	3:8–22
V.	On doing the will of God	4:1–19
VI.	Responsibilities in the church	5:1–11
VII.	Final greetings and blessing	5:12–14

WHERE? The letter was likely written from Rome, as indicated by the reference to Babylon (5:13), which the readers would have understood as a reference to Rome, and addressed to suffering Christians in Asia Minor.

WHEN? Perhaps written by Peter during Nero's persecution, (64 to 65 C.E.), it was more likely written during the time of Domitian (ca. 95 C.E.) or Trajan (ca. 112 C.E.).

WHY? Specifically, the writing offers consolation and encouragement to a suffering church. But 1 Peter has the more general theme of guiding Christians in ethical living that will please God and not offend neighbors.

Jude

The book of Jude was written to defend the "faith that was once for all entrusted to the saints" (v. 3).

WHO? Jude is a pseudonymous work addressed to a general church audience.

WHAT? The author harshly judges an unidentified group of false teachers and attempts to persuade the readers to join in the defense of Christian orthodoxy. This short book may be outlined as follows:

I.	Salutation	v.1
II.	The occasion for the letter	vv. 2–4
III.	The judgment on false teaching	vv. 5–15
IV.	Warnings and exhortation	vv. 17–23
V.	Benediction	vv. 24–25

WHERE AND WHEN? The letter was probably written from Rome in the early second century C.E.

WHY? Jude was written to counter false teachers who were threatening the faith of "true" Christians. The author of Jude is direct in his assertion that these false teachers will be subject to God's judgment.

2 Peter

The author of 2 Peter incorporates much of Jude into his writing, continues the warning against false teachers, and defends the apocalyptic hope of the return of Christ.

WHO? The author is unknown, and the letter is addressed to a general readership.

WHAT? The author attempts to establish his apostolic credentials (1:17–18) and then proceeds to attack false teachers who pervert the apostolic faith. The letter has the following structure:

I.	Salutation	1:1–2
II.	True knowledge of God	1:3–21
	A. A gift from God	1:3–4
	B. A part of experience	1:5–11
	C. Certainty of the truth	1:12–21
III.	The peril of false teaching	2:1–22
	A. The intrusion of error	2:1–10
	B. The judgment of error	2:11–22
IV.	The hope of true knowledge	3:1–18
	A. The Lord's coming	3:1–7
	B. Be patient	3:8–13
	C. Final exhortation	3:14–18

WHERE AND WHEN? The letter was most likely written from Rome as late as 140 C.E., making it the latest of the New Testament writings.

WHY? The author of 2 Peter writes to warn against false teachers. He connects his warning to the Parousia, which is both an encouragement to faithful Christians who persevere in the true faith and a time of judgment on good and evil.

1 John

1 John was written to counter a secession from the Christian community in Ephesus. This community is often referred to as the Johannine community named after the apostle John. First John establishes a set of criteria in order to distinguish between true and false belief. True faith is based on the incarnation of Jesus. He truly came as a human being in the flesh, not as one who merely appeared to be human.

WHO? The author, who is probably the author of 2 and 3 John as well, is not likely either the apostle John or the author of the Gospel of John, but a leader in the Johannine community. We know him as John the Elder.

WHAT? First John is a sermon *against* the schism in the Johannine community and *for* the incarnational character of true faith. The book's argument unfolds as follows:

I.	The ground of faith	1:1–4
II.	God is light	1:5–3:10
	A. So live in fellowship, obedience, and forgiveness	1:5–2:17
	B. And avoid false teaching	2:18–3:10
III.	God is love	3:11–5:12
	A. So love one another	3:11–24
	B. Test the spirits	4:1–6
	C. Love is the test	4:7–21
	D. Love means obedience	5:1–5
	E. True faith	5:6–12
IV.	Epilogue: sin and forgiveness	5:13–21

WHERE? The letter is addressed to Christians in Ephesus, the center of the Johannine community.

WHEN? The writing has been variously dated by scholars, but most place it after 90 C.E. and suggest a date between 95 and 110 C.E.

WHY? The author targets the schismatic group in the Johannine community that had begun to question that Jesus was truly human. He asserts a Christology that insists that the earthly Jesus and the heavenly Christ are the same being and that he was born in the flesh and truly suffered and died.

2 John

A short writing, 2 John echoes the themes of 1 John: truth (light), love, obedience, false teachers, and eternal life.

WHO? The author (John the Elder), likely the same person who wrote 1 John, addresses his remarks to a church in the Johannine community.

WHAT? The writer's purpose is to warn against "the anti-Christ" who teaches that Jesus was not a human being. Such teaching must be resisted, and love must hold a conflicted and threatened community together. Second John may be outlined as follows:

I.	Salutation	vv. 1–2
II.	The commandment to love and believe the true doctrine of Christ	vv. 3–11
III.	Final greetings	vv. 12–14

WHERE AND WHEN? The letter was written in the same time frame and location as 1 John.

WHY? The author of 2 John has pastoral concern and affection for the church ("elect lady") to which he writes. His concern is to warn the church against gnostic tendencies and to urge them to live in love.

3 John

In this short letter, the writer asks his friend Gaius to extend hospitality to some Christian workers led by Demetrius.

WHO? The author writes to his Christian friend Gaius in the Johannine community, and addresses a particular situation in the church that has caused some tension. The tension is caused by Diotrephes, who has not acknowledged the authority in the church. Demetrius, however, has been very hospitable.

WHAT? The letter reflects the schismatic tension in the Johannine community, and the particular problems caused by Diotrephes. The short letter has the following structure:

I.	Salutation	vv. 1–4
II.	Hospitality to strangers	vv. 5–8
III.	Condemnation of Diotrephes and commendation of Demetrius	vv. 9–12
IV.	Final greeting	vv. 13–15

WHERE AND WHEN? Again, John the Elder writes within and to the Johannine community toward the end of the first century C.E.

WHY? He writes to commend Gaius and urges him and his church to continue to be true to the faith and offer hospitality. There is a note of caution about Diotrephes, who is spreading false charges and does not welcome friends.

Revelation

The book of Revelation is generally placed in the literary genre called "apocalyptic," from the Greek word meaning "uncovering" or "disclosure." The book "reveals" unseen realities, both in heaven and on earth and places the current conditions on earth in cosmic perspective. Its message, articulated in the language of metaphor and symbol, is one of hope for suffering Christians.

WHO? The author identifies himself as John, who is writing in exile from the Aegean island of Patmos. His exile was caused by his Christian faith (1:9). According to the tradition, John was the son of Zebedee mentioned in the Gospels, but there is little evidence to support this view. Neither is the author John the Elder who lived in Ephesus about 100 C.E.

The central figure in Revelation is Jesus Christ, who is an all-powerful heavenly figure. John's Jesus is not the suffering servant of Mark or the Gospel of John's embodiment of divine wisdom but a warrior-king who does battle with his enemies and who will ultimately triumph (19:11–21).

WHAT? The message of Revelation is hope for suffering Christians and the counsel to persevere. The time is coming when the current evil will be checked. When Christ returns, the forces of evil will be vanquished and a new age will begin.

The theme is delivered in the form of visions, drawn largely from the Old Testament and from some noncanonical sources. The author's structure is complex, sufficiently so that the book has been variously interpreted. Some see in the visions a prediction of the end of the world, and others view the prophecies of Revelation as addressed to circumstances in the late first century. The book may be divided into nine major sections:

I.	Prologue: the author identifies himself and claims authority for his vision	1:1–20
II.	The letters of Jesus to the seven churches in Asia Minor	2:1–3:22
III.	The visions from heaven, the seven seals, and a scroll	4:1–8:5
IV.	The seven trumpets	8:6–11:19
V.	Signs from heaven: the woman, the dragon, the beast, the lamb, and the seven plagues	12:1–16:21
VI.	Visions of the "great whore" and the fall of Babylon (Rome)	17:1–18:24

VII. The final battle with evil and the vision
     of the end   19:1–20:15
VIII. The new heaven and the new earth   21:1–22:5
IX.   Epilogue and benediction   22:6–21

WHERE? John writes from Patmos, an island in the Aegean Sea, to Christians in Asia Minor. He mentions seven churches in Asia Minor:

Ephesus   2:1–7
Smyrna   2:8–11
Pergamum   2:12–17
Thyatira   2:18–29
Sardis   3:1–6
Philadelphia   3:7–13
Laodicea   3:14–22
(See Appendix B, fig. 11.)

WHEN? The book is generally dated near the end of the reign of the Roman Emperor Domitian, about 95 to 96 C.E.

WHY? The occasion for writing may have been a persecution initiated by Domitian. A direct persecution against the church is possible, although it is more likely that the churches in Asia Minor were subject to the sporadic repression common in the Roman Empire in the late first and early second centuries.

In order to sustain these Christians in the midst of their suffering, John writes to encourage them and urges them to remain faithful to Christ in their difficult circumstances. John is a realist about the power of Rome and the limitations within the churches. He sets the weakness of the churches in the face of the powerful Roman Empire over against the sovereign God, who will triumph over evil and promises ultimate justice and the riches of heaven.

APPENDIX A: SAMPLE TESTS

BIBLE CONTENT EXAM: 1991

Pentateuch

1. Who thought Israel would easily be able to overcome the Canaanites?
   a. Gershon
   b. Balaam
   c. Caleb
   d. Korah

2. According to the book of Deuteronomy, with what will God bless Israel?
   a. faithfulness
   b. purity
   c. righteousness
   d. prosperity

3. Which book contains the following statement: "If a man commits adultery with the wife of his neighbor, both the adulterer and the adulteress shall be put to death"?
   a. Genesis
   b. Exodus
   c. Leviticus
   d. Deuteronomy

4. In a conversation between which characters does this statement occur: "you will be like God, knowing good and evil"?
   a. God and Adam
   b. Moses and Zipporah
   c. Abraham and Sarah
   d. Eve and the snake

5. According to the book of Leviticus, which group is to purify themselves and make sacrifices on certain occasions?
   a. sojourners
   b. women
   c. soldiers
   d. servants

6. By what means were the Israelites guided through the wilderness after they left Egypt?
   a. Jethro and his family
   b. Moses' knowledge of the area
   c. the pillars of cloud and of fire
   d. the reconnaissance of the twelve spies

7. To whom were the laws in Leviticus delivered?
   a. Eleazar
   b. Aaron
   c. Joshua
   d. Moses

8. In the book of Deuteronomy, which statement follows "Hear, O Israel: the LORD our God is one LORD"?
   a. "You shall have no other gods before me."
   b. "And you shall love the LORD your God with all your heart."
   c. "And you shall remember all the ways which the LORD your God has led you."
   d. "You shall not put the LORD your God to the test."

9. With what event are the "scapegoat," "Aaron," and "sin offering" connected?
   a. Day of Atonement
   b. Feast of Harvest
   c. Feast of Ingathering
   d. Passover

10. Which statement accurately describes Melchizedek?
    a. He was king in Hebron.
    b. He was priest of God Most High.

c. He paid tithes to Abraham.
d. He joined Abraham in a military campaign.

11. Who said: "As for you, you meant evil against me; but God meant it for good"?
a. Cain
b. Lot
c. Joseph
d. Jacob

12. Who was made a leper but then healed after seven days?
a. Miriam
b. Jezebel
c. Vashti
d. Bathsheba

13. Who "went away from the presence of the LORD, and dwelt in the land of Nod, east of Eden"?
a. Abel
b. Adam
c. Cain
d. Enoch

14. What group was supposed to care for the tent of meeting?
a. the Levites
b. Korah and his family
c. Nadab and Abihu
d. the Reubenites

15. Who told Moses to choose "able men" to help ease the burden of his responsibilities?
a. God
b. Aaron
c. Jethro
d. Miriam

16. According to Numbers 34:6, what was to be the western boundary of the Promised Land?
a. the wilderness of Zin along the side of Edom
b. the Great Sea and its coast
c. from Azmon to the Brook of Egypt
d. from Zedad to Ziphron

17. Where was the passover instituted?
a. Egypt
b. the heights of Moab
c. Jericho
d. Peniel

Historical Books

18. Who are the three main characters in 1 Samuel?
a. Deborah, Gideon, and Samson
b. Samson, Saul, and Nathan
c. Samuel, Saul, and David
d. David, Jonathan, and Nathan

19. In the book of Esther, at whom is Mordecai angry?
a. Ahasuerus
b. Vashti
c. Haman
d. Hegai

20. Over what empire did Artaxerxes rule?
a. Babylon
b. Egypt
c. Greece
d. Persia

21. In which books does the prophet Elijah appear?
a. 1 and 2 Samuel
b. 1 and 2 Kings
c. 1 and 2 Chronicles
d. 1 Kings and 1 Chronicles

22. Who killed Sisera, commander of a Canaanite army?
a. a bear
b. a man
c. a lion
d. a woman

23. According to Joshua 4, what did the stones carried across the Jordan River represent?
a. the number of enemies Israel defeated in battle
b. the twelve tribes of Israel

c. the number of attempts to cross the Jordan River

d. twelve years of battle

24. In the story involving what main character do "Bethlehem," "Naomi," and "barley harvest" all play a role?
    a. Esther
    b. Ruth
    c. Samuel
    d. Saul

25. Under whose leadership were the walls of Jerusalem rebuilt?
    a. Ezra
    b. Nehemiah
    c. Joshua
    d. Zerubbabel

26. According to 1 Chronicles, what is David not allowed to build?
    a. a garden
    b. a temple
    c. a water tunnel
    d. a wall around Jerusalem

27. What were Shamgar, Gideon, and Jephthah?
    a. judges
    b. princes
    c. singers
    d. priests

28. According to Joshua 2, what did Rahab do?
    a. hid Israelite spies
    b. helped the men of Jericho prepare for war
    c. hid soldiers for the king
    d. warned the city of enemy attack

29. In the story involving what main character do "the four hundred prophets of Asherah," "Mount Carmel," and "Ahab" appear?
    a. Elijah
    b. Elisha

c. Micah
d. Obadiah

30. What king said to Nathan the prophet, "See now, I dwell in a house of cedar, but the ark of God dwells in a tent"?
    a. Saul
    b. David
    c. Solomon
    d. Hezekiah

Prophets

31. What was the name of Jeremiah's scribe?
    a. Benaiah
    b. Balaam
    c. Baruch
    d. Benjamin

32. During whose reign did Haggai appear as a prophet?
    a. Hezekiah
    b. Josiah
    c. Nebuchadnezzar
    d. Darius

33. In which book does the following quotation appear: "He has showed you, O man, what is good; and what does the LORD require of you but to do justice, and to love kindness, and to walk humbly with your God"?
    a. Ezekiel
    b. Hosea
    c. Micah
    d. Zechariah

34. Who declared, "I am no prophet, nor a prophet's son"?
    a. Joel
    b. Amos
    c. Micah
    d. Habakkuk

35. In which book does the following quotation appear: "How lonely sits the city that was full of people! How like a widow has she become, she that was great among the nations! She that was a princess among the cities has become a vassal"?
   a. Isaiah
   b. Jeremiah
   c. Lamentations
   d. Ezekiel

36. What statement describes what Isaiah says about the wolf and lamb, leopard and kid, calf and lion?
   a. "Be fruitful and multiply."
   b. "They shall not hurt or destroy in all my holy mountain."
   c. "Thou hast given them dominion over the works of thy hands."
   d. "Wild oxen shall fall with them, and young steers with the mighty bulls."

37. Who brought Jeremiah from the dungeon to ask him, "Is there any word from the LORD?"
   a. the king
   b. princes of Judah
   c. Baruch
   d. Gedaliah

38. Which book contains many passages concerning "my servant"?
   a. Amos
   b. Ezekiel
   c. Isaiah
   d. Jeremiah

39. Which prophet was directed by God to name his children "Jezreel," "Not pitied," and "Not my people"?
   a. Ezekiel
   b. Hosea

   c. Joel
   d. Amos

40. How were the words, which Daniel interpreted ("MENE, MENE, TEKEL, PARSIN"), conveyed?
   a. spoken by a messenger of God
   b. spoken by Daniel
   c. read by an eunuch
   d. written on a wall

41. Of whom is it reported, "the men knew that he was fleeing from the presence of the LORD"?
   a. Hosea
   b. Joel
   c. Obadiah
   d. Jonah

42. In which book does the following statement occur: "And he said to me, 'Son of man, stand upon your feet, and I will speak with you . . . . I send you to the people of Israel, to a nation of rebels, who have rebelled against me' "?
   a. Daniel
   b. Ezekiel
   c. Hosea
   d. Jonah

43. In which book do the following quotations occur: "the righteous shall live by his faith," "the earth will be filled with the knowledge of the glory of the LORD," and "in wrath remember mercy"?
   a. Hosea
   b. Amos
   c. Micah
   d. Habakkuk

44. For an example of the story of the call of a prophet, to which book would one turn?
   a. Ezekiel
   b. Joel
   c. Zechariah
   d. Malachi

45. In which book do these lines appear: "Before I formed you in the womb I knew you"; "Cursed be the day on which I was born"; "Is there no balm in Gilead?"
    a. Ezekiel
    b. Hosea
    c. Joel
    d. Jeremiah

46. Which book contains the following lines, "In the wilderness prepare the way of the LORD," "He will feed his flock like a shepherd"?
    a. Daniel
    b. Amos
    c. Hosea
    d. Isaiah

47. Which passage appears in the book of Joel?
    a. "Come now, let us reason together, says the LORD: though your sins are like scarlet, they shall be as white as snow."
    b. "Your sons and your daughters shall prophesy, your old men shall dream dreams, and your young men shall see visions."
    c. "Behold, a young woman shall conceive, and bear a son, and shall call his name Immanuel."
    d. "The earth shall be full of the knowledge of the LORD, as the waters cover the sea."

Psalms and Wisdom Literature

48. In what book does the following quotation appear: "There was a day when the sons of God came to present themselves before the LORD, and Satan also came among them"?
    a. Ecclesiastes
    b. Job
    c. Proverbs
    d. Psalms

49. Which statement does Proverbs 31 *not* include as a description of "a good wife"?
    a. "Her children rise up and call her blessed."
    b. "She opens her mouth with wisdom, and the teaching of kindness is on her tongue."
    c. "For your love is better than wine, your anointing oils are fragrant."
    d. "Charm is deceitful, and beauty is vain, but a woman who fears the LORD is to be praised."

50. In what book does the following quotation occur, "But behold, this also was vanity"?
    a. Job
    b. Proverbs
    c. Ecclesiastes
    d. Lamentations

51. What book concludes with the following verse, "Make haste, my beloved, and be like a gazelle or a young stag upon the mountains of spices"?
    a. Job
    b. Proverbs
    c. Ecclesiastes
    d. Song of Solomon

52. Which statement or theme characterizes Psalm 91?
    a. God's law
    b. the folly of human sin
    c. the establishment of covenant
    d. the power and protection of God

53. In which book does the following quotation appear: "Shall a faultfinder contend with the Almighty? He who argues with God, let him answer it"?
    a. Job
    b. Psalms
    c. Proverbs
    d. Ecclesiastes

54. In the book of Job, who says, "Do you still hold fast your integrity? Curse God, and die"?
    a. Job's wife
    b. one of Job's daughters
    c. Zophar
    d. Elihu

55. With what phrase does the following proverb conclude: "Train up a child in the way he should go, and when he is old he will not . . ."?
    a. depart from it
    b. despise you
    c. dishonor your name
    d. turn aside to evil

56. With what lines does Psalm 51 begin?
    a. "The almighty God, the LORD speaks . . ."
    b. "Have mercy upon me, O God, according to thy steadfast love."
    c. "Make a joyful noise to God."
    d. "The LORD reigns, he is robed with majesty."

57. What is the first line in Psalm 1?
    a. "Blessed is the man who walks not in the counsel of the wicked . . ."
    b. "O LORD, our LORD, how majestic is thy name in all the earth!"
    c. "The earth is the LORD's and the fullness thereof . . ."
    d. "The heavens are telling the glory of God; and the firmament proclaims his handiwork."

Synoptic Gospels

58. According to Matthew, Mark, and Luke, why did Herod arrest John the Baptist?
    a. John reproached him for living opulently.
    b. John accused him of adultery.
    c. John accused him of disloyalty to his own people.
    d. John accused him of using Roman troops to quell Jewish uprisings.

59. In which book or books is the story of the shepherds "keeping . . . their flock by night" found?
    a. Matthew
    b. Mark
    c. Luke
    d. Matthew and Luke

60. According to Matthew, what does the name of the child, "Emman-uel," born to Mary, mean?
    a. "He will save his people from their sins."
    b. "He will govern my people Israel."
    c. "The people who sat in darkness have seen a great light."
    d. "God with us."

61. According to Mark, what does the angel tell the women at the empty tomb?
    a. to wait in Jerusalem, where Jesus will appear first to Peter, then to the twelve, and then to the whole company of disciples
    b. to wait in Jerusalem until Jesus appears to Mary his mother
    c. to tell his disciples and Peter that he is going before them

and the women to Galilee; there they will all see him, just as Jesus had told them

d. to tell Mary, Jesus' mother, to wait at the tomb until Jesus appears to her

62. Which Gospel or Gospels open with a genealogy?
a. Matthew
b. Mark
c. Luke
d. Mark and Luke

63. About whom, and on what occasion, was it said, "Certainly you are one of them; for you are a Galilean"?
a. Joseph of Arimathea when he asked for Jesus' body
b. Peter, in the courtyard of the high priest
c. John, preaching in Jordan
d. Stephen, preaching in Jerusalem

64. According to Luke, at which moment did the disciples who journeyed to Emmaus recognize Jesus?
a. when he opened the scriptures
b. when he gave them the Holy Spirit
c. when he showed them the nail prints in his hands
d. when he broke bread and gave it to them

65. In which Synoptic Gospel or Gospels are the Beatitudes found?
a. Matthew and Luke
b. Mark and Luke
c. Mark and Matthew
d. Luke

66. According to both the Gospels of Mark and Matthew, what did Jesus say from the cross?
a. "Father, forgive them for they know not what they do."
b. "Father, into thy hands I commend my spirit."
c. "I thirst."
d. "My God, my God, why hast thou forsaken me?"

67. About whom did Jesus say that his or her action should be remembered wherever the gospel is preached?
a. the woman who had the flow of blood
b. the woman who poured ointment on Jesus' head
c. the centurion who declared Jesus was the Son of God
d. the Samaritan in the parable

68. What did the angel promise Zechariah, when he was praying in the Temple?
a. a son
b. a daughter
c. healing
d. salvation

69. How does Jesus answer the question, "Who are my mother and my brothers?"
a. I have no mother or brothers.
b. those who have always been my mother and my brothers
c. those who follow me faithfully
d. whoever does the will of God

70. What did the householder say when many excused themselves from the householder's great banquet?
a. "How hard it is for the wealthy to enter the kingdom of heaven."
b. "Bring in the poor and maimed and blind and lame."

c. "Finally I will send my son; him they will respect."

d. "Never again shall I drink from the fruit of the vine until the day when the kingdom of God comes."

Johannine Writings

71. Which statement is *not* characteristic of the Gospel of John?
    a. "He who does what is true comes to the light."
    b. "No one has ever seen God: the only Son, who is in the bosom of the Father, he has made him known."
    c. "They cried out, 'You are the son of God.' And he strictly ordered them not to make him known."
    d. "That which is born of the flesh is flesh, and that which is born of the Spirit is Spirit."

72. How is this phrase in John 1 completed: "And the Word became flesh and . . ."?
    a. his name was called Jesus
    b. increased in wisdom and in stature and in favor with God and man
    c. his name was called Immanuel
    d. dwelt among us, full of grace and truth

73. According to the Gospel of John, why was the Gospel written?
    a. so "that you may believe that Jesus is the Christ, the Son of God, and that believing you may have life in his name"
    b. to present "an orderly account for you . . . that you may know the truth concerning the things of which you have been informed"

c. so "that your joy may be complete"

d. to present "the book of the genealogy of Jesus Christ, the Son of David, the Son of Abraham"

74. Which of the following is an important theme of the First Letter of John?
    a. election
    b. creation
    c. predestination
    d. love

75. According to the book of Revelation, where was John when he heard "a loud voice like a trumpet"?
    a. praying on a high mountain
    b. worshiping in the Temple
    c. suffering persecution in Ephesus
    d. staying on the island of Patmos

76. What does the book of Revelation *not* include?
    a. a vision of a woman clothed with the sun
    b. a vision of four horsemen
    c. a vision of the glorified Christ
    d. a vision of Jesus with Moses and Elijah

Acts and Pauline Writings

77. Who was Onesimus?
    a. a disciple
    b. a soldier
    c. a politician
    d. a slave

78. Why does Paul refer to Abraham in his letter to the Romans?
    a. Since Abraham was circumcised, all should be circumcised.
    b. Justification by faith is exemplified by Abraham, since

he received the promise by faith before he was circumcised.

c. As Abraham was a wanderer and sojourner, so Christians are pilgrims and sojourners in this world.

d. The promise made to Abraham is now extended to the Gentiles and is no longer valid for Jews.

79. On what does Paul base his order to the church of the Thessalonians: "If anyone will not work, let him not eat"?
a. "Do not, for the sake of food, destroy the work of God."
b. "I know your works; you have the name of being alive, and you are dead."
c. "What does it profit, my brethren, if a man says he has faith but has not works?"
d. "For you yourselves know how you ought to imitate us; we were not idle when we were with you."

80. According to the book of Ephesians, what is God's ultimate plan for "the fullness of time"?
a. to baptize all nations
b. to convince all the earth to praise God
c. to make every tongue confess Jesus as Lord
d. to unite all things in Christ

81. In 2 Corinthians, how is Paul's statement "Therefore, if any one is in Christ . . ." completed?
a. he should be baptized
b. he will uphold Christ's law
c. he is a new creation
d. he will turn from the law

82. In what context within 1 Corinthians does Paul write about "the body of Christ"?
a. in a discussion of the resurrection
b. in a discussion of spiritual gifts
c. in a discussion of marital ethics
d. in a discussion of apostolic authority

83. In Galatians, what does Paul claim is the source of his gospel?
a. personal reflection
b. a revelation of Jesus Christ
c. the apostles in Jerusalem
d. an event on the Damascus road

84. What should those who speak "in a tongue" pray for?
a. the power to heal
b. the power to interpret
c. the power to exorcise demons
d. the power to convert

85. For whom did Paul take up "a contribution"?
a. the Christians at Boroea
b. the church at Rome
c. the people of Athens
d. the poor saints of Jerusalem

86. What is one of the central concerns in 1 Timothy?
a. children
b. drunkards
c. the rich
d. widows

87. Who addressed the men of Judea at Pentecost?
a. James
b. Peter
c. Paul
d. Stephen

88. To which church did Paul write a letter before visiting them?
a. Athens
b. Corinth

c. Philippi

d. Rome

89. Which statement best summarizes Paul's argument in Romans that there is no difference between Jew and Greek?

a. They all need milk, not solid food.

b. They have sinned and come short.

c. They have this treasure in earthen vessels.

d. They are the temple of the living God.

90. What is Paul's situation at the end of Acts?

a. He is under house arrest in Rome.

b. He is on trial for his life.

c. He is in jail in Corinth.

d. He is on his way to Spain.

91. According to Acts, from what city did Saul come?

a. Antioch

b. Athens

c. Jerusalem

d. Tarsus

92. What is Paul's situation when he writes to those in Philippi?

a. He is on a ship.

b. He is in prison.

c. He is traveling in Spain.

d. He is preaching in Corinth.

93. Who said, and in what situation, "I have no silver and gold, but I give you what I have"?

a. Peter to the lame man at the Beautiful Gate of the Temple

b. Peter to Simon Magnus, who wanted to buy the Holy Spirit

c. Paul to Felix, who "hoped that money would be given him by Paul"

d. Paul to the owners of the soothsaying girl in Philippi

Rest of the New Testament

94. In which book does this quotation appear: "And convince some, who doubt; save some, by snatching them out of the fire; on some have mercy with fear"?

a. Hebrews

b. James

c. 2 Peter

d. Jude

95. In which book does the following quotation appear: "If a brother or sister is ill-clad and in lack of daily food, and one of you says to them, 'Go in peace, be warmed and filled,' without giving them the things needed for the body, what does it profit?"

a. Hebrews

b. James

c. Jude

d. 2 Peter

96. According to 1 Peter, what should be the Christian attitude toward every human institution?

a. They should oppose it.

b. They should question it.

c. They should withdraw from it.

d. They should be subject to it.

97. Which book refers to the early Christian practice of praying over the sick and anointing them with oil?

a. Hebrews

b. James

c. 1 Peter

d. 2 Peter

98. In what way does the letter to the Hebrews describe faith?

a. "Because we are justified by faith, we have peace with God."

b. "Christ may dwell in your hearts through faith."

c. "Now faith is the assurance of things hoped for, the conviction of things not seen."
d. "Faith apart from works is dead."

99. With what issue is the following quotation from 2 Peter concerned: "With the LORD one day is like a thousand years, and a thousand years are one day"?
a. the persistence of evil
b. God's work as creator
c. the millennium
d. the apparent delay of Christ's return

100. Why does the author of Hebrews think Melchizedek is important?
a. Like Jesus, he suffered for the sins of others.
b. He is a type of Jesus' eternal kingship.
c. As a Gentile, he represents the mission to the Gentiles.
d. He is a "likeness" of Jesus' priestly work.

BIBLE CONTENT EXAM: 1991
Answer Sheet

Pentateuch

1. c. Numbers 13
2. d. Deuteronomy 11:13ff.
3. c. Leviticus 20:10
4. d. Genesis 3:5
5. b. Leviticus 12:1–8
6. c. Exodus 13:21–22
7. d. Leviticus 1:1
8. b. Deuteronomy 6:5
9. a. Leviticus 16
10. b. Genesis 14:18
11. c. Genesis 50:20
12. a. Numbers 12:10–15
13. c. Genesis 4:16
14. a. Numbers 18:23
15. c. Exodus 18:17–23
16. b. Numbers 34:6
17. a. Exodus 11–13

Historical Books

18. c. 1 Samuel
19. c. Esther 3:2
20. d. Ezra 7:13
21. b. 1 Kings 17—19, 2 Kings 2
22. d. Judges 4:21
23. b. Joshua 4:1–5
24. b. Ruth 1 and 2
25. b. Nehemiah 2—3
26. b. 1 Chronicles 22:8
27. a. Judges 3:31, 6, 8; 11—12
28. a. Joshua 2:1–11
29. a. 1 Kings 18:17–19
30. b. 2 Samuel 7:2

Prophets

31. c. Jeremiah 36
32. d. Haggai 1:1
33. c. Micah 6:8
34. b. Amos 7:14
35. c. Lamentations 1:1
36. b. Isaiah 11:9
37. a. Jeremiah 37:16–17
38. c. Isaiah 40—55
39. b. Hosea 1:4, 6, 9
40. d. Daniel 5:5, 24–25
41. d. Jonah 1:10

42. b. Ezekiel 2:1, 3
43. d. Habakkuk 2:4, 14; 3:2
44. a. Ezekiel 1:1–28
45. d. Jeremiah 1:5; 20:14; 8:22
46. d. Isaiah 40:3, 11
47. b. Joel 2:28

Psalms and Wisdom Literature

48. b. Job 1:6
49. c. Proverbs 31:26, 28, 30; Song of Solomon 1:2–3
50. c. Ecclesiastics 2:1
51. d. Song of Solomon 8:14
52. d. Psalm 91
53. a. Job 40:2
54. a. Job 2:9
55. a. Proverbs 22:6
56. b. Psalm 51:1
57. a. Psalm 1:1

Synoptic Gospels

58. b. Matthew 14:3–4; Mark 6:17–18; Luke 3:19–20
59. c. Luke 2:8
60. d. Matthew 1:23
61. c. Mark 16:7
62. a. Matthew 1:1–17
63. b. Mark 14:70
64. d. Luke 24:30
65. a. Matthew 5:3–12; Luke 6:20–23
66. d. Matthew 27:46; Mark 15:34
67. b. Matthew 26:13
68. a. Luke 1:13
69. d. Mark 3:35
70. b. Luke 14:21

Johannine Writings

71. c. Mark 3:11
72. d. John 1:14
73. a. John 20:31
74. d. 1 John 2:7–11
75. d. Revelation 1:9–10
76. d. Revelation 5:6–14; 6:2–8; 12:1

Acts and Pauline Writings

77. d. Philemon 10
78. b. Romans 4:11
79. d. 2 Thessalonians 3:7, 10
80. d. Ephesians 1:9–10
81. c. 2 Corinthians 5:17
82. b. 1 Corinthians 12
83. b. Galatians 1:12
84. b. 1 Corinthians 14:13
85. d. 2 Corinthians 9:1
86. d. 1 Timothy 5:3
87. b. Acts 2:14
88. d. Romans 1:13
89. b. Romans 3:23
90. a. Acts 28:17–28
91. d. Acts 9:11
92. b. Philemon 1:13–14
93. a. Acts 3:6

Rest of the New Testament

94. d. Jude 22, 23
95. b. James 2:15–16
96. d. 1 Peter 2:13
97. b. James 5:14
98. c. Hebrews 11:1
99. c. 2 Peter 3:4–10
100. d. Hebrews 6:20; 7:15

BIBLE CONTENT EXAM: 1992

Pentateuch

1. How did the people of Israel corrupt themselves while Moses was on the mountain with the Lord?
   a. They sacrificed to Baal.
   b. They offered strange fire to the Lord.
   c. They turned to Balaam to lead them in a new way.
   d. They made a molten calf, worshiped it, and sacrificed to it.

2. Israelite law demanded scrupulous care in the treatment of the blood of slain animals. What reason for this is given in Leviticus?
   a. Blood is holy.
   b. Blood is inedible.
   c. Blood is life.
   d. Blood is the choicest part of the animal.

3. Who did the Lord command Moses to bring near to him "to serve me as priests"?
   a. Aaron and his sons
   b. Jethro and his brothers
   c. Joshua and his brothers
   d. Rechabites

4. How many sons did Jacob have?
   a. six
   b. eight
   c. ten
   d. twelve

5. Which of the following statements is not a part of the conversation between God and Moses at the burning bush?
   a. God: "I have seen the affliction of my people . . ."
   b. God: "Put off your shoes from your feet, for the place on which you are standing is holy ground."
   c. Moses: "And they ask me, 'What is his name?' what shall I say to them?"
   d. God: "You shall have no other gods before me."

6. What is the focus of the conversation between Eve and the serpent?
   a. apples
   b. covenant
   c. death
   d. tilling the soil

7. The Ten Commandments are recorded in which two books?
   a. Genesis and Numbers
   b. Exodus and Numbers
   c. Exodus and Deuteronomy
   d. Numbers and Deuteronomy

8. Of which of the following was Jethro a priest?
   a. Bethel
   b. Midian
   c. Moab
   d. Ur of the Chaldees

9. What accompanied the giving of the Ten Commandments to Moses?
   a. a deep silence
   b. a heavenly chorus
   c. the songs of the people
   d. thunder and lightning

10. Who did the Lord name when Moses, nearing death, asked for a man to be his successor?
    a. Aaron the brother of Moses
    b. Caleb the son of Jephunneh
    c. Eleazar the priest
    d. Joshua son of Nun

11. In what way was Miriam punished for speaking against Moses?
    a. She contracted leprosy.

b. She was banished from the camp.
c. She was declared unclean.
d. She was removed from her leadership position.

12. Who said, "Am I my brother's keeper?"
    a. Abel
    b. Cain
    c. Isaac
    d. Joseph

13. What was the sign of the covenant God made with Noah and his descendants?
    a. God placed a bow in the clouds.
    b. Noah became the first tiller of the soil.
    c. The ark would carry his family through the flood.
    d. The rain came to a halt.

14. What is the first of the Ten Commandments?
    a. "Honor your father and your mother, that your days may be long in the land which the LORD your God gives you."
    b. "Remember the sabbath day, to keep it holy."
    c. "You shall have no other gods before me."
    d. "You shall not take the name of the LORD your God in vain."

15. What resulted from the mission of the twelve spies?
    a. Israel remained in the wilderness for forty years.
    b. Miriam sang a song of victory to the Lord.
    c. The rod of Aaron sprouted forth buds and bore ripe almonds.
    d. the stoning of Caleb

16. Which of the following phrases is used as a synonym for the Promised Land?
    a. a land flowing with milk and honey
    b. a land of blood and tears
    c. a land of hills and rivers
    d. Palestine

17. What was the sign of the covenant God made with Abraham and his descendants?
    a. that Abraham must leave Ur of the Chaldeans
    b. the birth of Ishmael
    c. the circumcision of every male in his house and any of his descendants
    d. the overthrow of Sodom and Gomorrah

Historical Books

18. Where did Joshua send two men as spies?
    a. Gilgal
    b. Jericho
    c. Lebanon
    d. Shittim

19. "Bring me a sword and divide the living child in two" occurs in a story that illustrates which of the following?
    a. Abner's desire for revenge
    b. Benaiah's loyalty to Solomon
    c. Joab's blood-thirstiness
    d. Solomon's wisdom

20. How many times did the seven priests, blowing rams' horns, march around the city of Jericho?
    a. one
    b. six
    c. seven
    d. twelve

21. What book contains the following quotation: "In those days there was no king in Israel; every man did what was right in his own eyes"?
    a. Joshua
    b. Judges
    c. Ruth
    d. 1 Samuel

22. The four hundred prophets of Asherah, Mount Carmel, and Ahab are parts of the story involving which of the following?
    a. Elijah
    b. Elisha
    c. Jezreel
    d. Micaiah son of Imlah

23. Which of the following was a judge?
    a. Deborah
    b. Miriam
    c. Naomi
    d. Ruth

24. "But will God indeed dwell on the earth? Behold, heaven and the highest heaven cannot contain thee; how much less this house which I have built!" Who spoke these words?
    a. David
    b. Ezra
    c. Hezekiah
    d. Solomon

25. Who was the father of Obed, "the father of Jesse, the father of David"?
    a. Boaz
    b. Hezron
    c. Perez
    d. Ram

26. "I will give you the vineyard of Naboth the Jezreelite." Who spoke these words?
    a. Ahasuerus to Esther
    b. Jezebel to Ahab

    c. Samson to Delilah
    d. Saul to David

27. What judge, "a Nazirite to God from birth," would "begin to deliver Israel from the hand of the Philistines"?
    a. Ehud
    b. Gideon
    c. Jephthah
    d. Samson

28. In Joshua, Rahab, who saved the spies, bound what to the window?
    a. brass snake
    b. golden ball
    c. scarlet cord
    d. trumpet

29. Who was king when a "book of the law" was found during Temple repairs?
    a. Ahab
    b. Joash
    c. Josiah
    d. Solomon

Prophets

30. Which prophet refused to eat the food of the Babylonian king while living at the Babylonian court?
    a. Jeremiah
    b. Ezekiel
    c. Daniel
    d. Jonah

31. Which book contains the vision of a new covenant to be written on the hearts of God's people?
    a. Jeremiah
    b. Amos
    c. Hosea
    d. Zephaniah

32. "As I was among the exiles by the river Chebar, the heavens were opened and I saw visions of God." To which prophet does this refer?
    a. Jeremiah
    b. Ezekiel

c. Daniel

d. Amos

33. In which prophetic book does the following quotation appear: "For to us a child is born, to us a son is given; and the government will be upon his shoulder"?

a. Isaiah

b. Ezekiel

c. Hosea

d. Amos

34. What prophet had a vision of a valley of dry bones?

a. Isaiah

b. Ezekiel

c. Amos

d. Zechariah

35. "I have found among the exiles from Judah a man who can make known to the king the interpretation." Regarding which prophet was this statement made?

a. Isaiah

b. Jeremiah

c. Daniel

d. Amos

36. Who named his children "Not pitied" and "Not my people" as signs of his message from God to Israel?

a. Isaiah

b. Jeremiah

c. Ezekiel

d. Hosea

37. To which prophet did the word of the Lord come, saying: "Before I formed you in the womb I knew you, and before you were born I consecrated you"?

a. Jeremiah

b. Ezekiel

c. Hosea

d. Amos

38. Which prophet declared: "Yet forty days, and Nineveh shall be overthrown"?

a. Ezekiel

b. Hosea

c. Joel

d. Jonah

39. Which prophet complained that God seduced him, overpowered him, and made him the butt of everyone's jokes?

a. Jeremiah

b. Hosea

c. Amos

d. Micah

40. What was Nehemiah commissioned to do?

a. raise an army to attack Sanballat

b. rebuild the Temple

c. rebuild the walls of Jerusalem

d. take the title of king of Israel

41. Which book contains the following quotation: "And he said to me, 'Son of man, stand upon your feet, and I will speak with you. . . . I send you to the people of Israel, to a nation of rebels, who have rebelled against me' "?

a. Ezekiel

b. Daniel

c. Jonah

d. Micah

42. Which prophet was thrown overboard by shipmates because the prophet told them the stormy sea had come about because of him?

a. Jeremiah

b. Ezekiel

c. Hosea

d. Jonah

43. Which book contains the following quotation: "I heard the voice of the LORD saying, 'Whom shall I send, and who will go for us?' Then I said, 'Here am I! Send me'"?
    a. Isaiah
    b. Jeremiah
    c. Lamentations
    d. Jonah

44. Which prophet said that what the Lord required was "to do justice, and to love kindness, and to walk humbly with your God"?
    a. Isaiah
    b. Jeremiah
    c. Amos
    d. Micah

45. Which prophet was commanded, "Son of man, eat what is offered to you; eat this scroll, and go, speak to the house of Israel"?
    a. Isaiah
    b. Ezekiel
    c. Jonah
    d. Micah

46. Which prophetic book envisions a future in which "your sons and daughters shall prophecy, your old men shall dream dreams, and your young men shall see visions"?
    a. Joel
    b. Haggai
    c. Zechariah
    d. Malachi

47. Which prophet was in prison during the Babylonian siege of Jerusalem?
    a. Isaiah
    b. Jeremiah
    c. Hosea
    d. Joel

Psalms and Wisdom Literature

48. Which of the following completes the quotation from Proverbs: "A soft answer turns away wrath, but a harsh word . . ."?
    a. accomplishes much
    b. captures attention
    c. enjoys obedience
    d. stirs up anger

49. Which of the following completes the quotation from Proverbs: "A good name is to be chosen rather than . . ."?
    a. acclaim of kings
    b. great riches
    c. high position
    d. soundness of body

50. "There was a day when the sons of God came to present themselves before the LORD, and Satan also came among them." In which book are these words written?
    a. Job
    b. Psalms
    c. Proverbs
    d. Ecclesiastes

51. Which of the following completes the quotation from Proverbs: "Train up a child in the way he should go and when he is old, he will . . ."?
    a. learn the ways of God
    b. not depart from it
    c. not lack for friends
    d. praise you

52. Which of the following completes the quotation from Psalms: "For as high as the heaven is above the earth . . ."?
    a. he has not dealt with us according to our sins

b. so great is his steadfast love toward those that fear him

c. so the LORD remembers that we are dust

d. the LORD works vindication and justice for all who are oppressed

53. "Let the words of my mouth, and the meditation of my heart be acceptable in thy sight, O LORD, my rock and my redeemer." Which book contains these words?
a. Psalms
b. Proverbs
c. Ecclesiastes
d. Song of Solomon

54. What book contains "a time for every matter under heaven"?
a. Psalms
b. Proverbs
c. Ecclesiastes
d. Lamentations

55. Which of the following completes the challenge of Satan to God regarding Job: ". . . put forth thy hand now, and touch his bone and his flesh, and he will . . ."?
a. be made whole
b. curse thee to thy face
c. proclaim thy presence
d. question thy mercy

56. Which of the following completes the quotation from Proverbs: "The fear of the LORD is the beginning of . . ."?
a. blessing
b. humility
c. wisdom
d. worship

57. Which of the following completes the quotation from Psalms: "God is our refuge and strength . . ."?
a. a very present help in trouble
b. Be still and know that I am God.

c. The Lord of hosts is with us.
d. The God of Jacob is our refuge.

Synoptic Gospels

58. Which two of Jesus' disciples were sons of Zebedee?
a. James and John
b. Peter and John
c. Simon and Andrew
d. Simon and James

59. According to Luke, what happened to Jesus after he preached in the synagogue of Nazareth?
a. He was asked to return.
b. He was invited to a banquet.
c. He was put out of the city.
d. He was taken to his mother's home.

60. Which of the following teachings is not found in Matthew?
a. "Blessed are the poor in spirit."
b. "You are Peter, and on this rock I will build my church."
c. "Woe to you, scribes and Pharisees, hypocrites."
d. "Remember Lot's wife."

61. In what town or city did Jesus grow up?
a. Bethlehem
b. Capernaum
c. Jerusalem
d. Nazareth

62. In Luke, who says, "LORD, now lettest thou thy servant depart in peace, according to thy word; for mine eyes have seen thy salvation which thou hast prepared in the presence of all peoples, a light for revelation to the Gentiles, and for glory to thy people Israel"?
a. Anna
b. Elizabeth

c. Simeon
d. Zechariah

63. What region was home base for Jesus' ministry?
a. Galilee
b. Judaea
c. Peraea
d. Samaria

64. Which of these statements is found in the first chapter of Matthew?
a. "A virgin shall conceive and bear a son."
b. "Glory to God in the highest."
c. "We had hoped that he was the one to redeem Israel."
d. "You are the Christ."

65. What did the woman who had a flow of blood for twelve years believe would bring about her healing?
a. persuading the disciples to help her
b. standing in Jesus' shadow when he walked past
c. stepping into the pool of Bethsaida
d. touching Jesus' clothing

66. What was Gethsemane?
a. a hill where Jesus was crucified
b. a valley where garbage was burned
c. a garden where Jesus prayed
d. a village where Jesus borrowed a colt

67. According to Matthew, Mark, and Luke, what did Jesus do just after he was baptized?
a. He called the twelve disciples.
b. He returned to Galilee.
c. He returned to Nazareth to tell his family.
d. He went into the wilderness [to be tempted].

68. When asked which commandment is greatest, Jesus answered, "You shall love the LORD your God with all your heart, and with all your soul, and with all your mind." What did he say was the second commandment?
a. "You shall love your neighbor as yourself."
b. "You shall not make for yourself a graven image."
c. "You shall have no other gods before me."
d. "Honor your father and your mother."

69. Which of the following correctly completes the statement: "For the Son of Man also came not to be served, but to serve . . ."?
a. and to build his church
b. and to heal the sick and cast out demons
c. and to give his life as a ransom for many
d. and to teach the ways of God

70. How is the following saying of Jesus completed: "And I tell you, you are Peter . . ."?
a. and on this rock I will build my church
b. and before the cock crows you will deny me three times
c. and I will make you fish for people
d. so watch here while I go and pray

Johannine Writings

71. Who was John the Baptist?
a. a disciple of Jesus
b. a prophet sent from Elijah
c. the one who came to bear witness to the light
d. the one who was with God from the beginning

72. Which of the following is an essential theme of the First Letter of John?
    a. election
    b. creation
    c. predestination
    d. love

73. Which of the following does *not* occur in Revelation?
    a. letters to seven churches
    b. a vision of a woman clothed with the sun
    c. a vision of four horsemen
    d. a vision of Jesus with Moses and Elijah

74. What special favor did Mary and Martha ask from Jesus?
    a. to care for them in their old age
    b. to celebrate Passover in their house
    c. to heal their brother, Lazarus
    d. to sit at Jesus' feet

75. " 'I am the Alpha and the Omega,' says the LORD God, 'who is and who was and who is to come, the Almighty.' " What book contains these words?
    a. John
    b. 1 John
    c. 3 John
    d. Revelation

76. What did John say when he saw Jesus coming to be baptized?
    a. "Behold, the lamb of God, who takes away the sin of the world."
    b. "Blessed be the LORD God of Israel, for he has visited and redeemed his people."
    c. "LORD, now lettest thou thy servant depart in peace . . . for mine eyes have seen thy salvation."
    d. "This is my beloved son in whom I am well pleased."

Acts and Pauline Writings

77. What book or letter contains an account of the day of Pentecost?
    a. Acts
    b. Romans
    c. 1 Corinthians
    d. Ephesians

78. Who was struck dead after trying to deceive Peter by hiding some of the money from the sale of a piece of property?
    a. Ananias and Sapphira
    b. Aquila and Priscilla
    c. Barnabas
    d. Lydia

79. "Since all have sinned and fall short of the glory of God, they are justified by his grace as a gift and through the redemption which is in Christ Jesus." In which of the following is this statement a theme?
    a. Paul's letter to Rome
    b. Paul's sermon at Mars Hill
    c. Peter's sermon at Pentecost
    d. Stephen's sermon

80. Which of the following baptized the "Ethiopian eunuch"?
    a. Barnabas
    b. Peter
    c. Philip
    d. Stephen

81. Who was on his way to Damascus when he heard a voice that said, "Why do you persecute me?"
    a. Barnabas
    b. Peter
    c. Philip
    d. Saul

82. Paul's statement, "For in Christ Jesus neither circumcision nor uncircumcision is of any avail, but faith working through love," characterizes his exhortations in what letter?
    a. 1 Corinthians
    b. Galatians
    c. Ephesians
    d. Colossians

83. How does Paul answer the question, "Are we to continue in sin that grace may abound?"
    a. "By no means. How can we who died to sin still live in it?"
    b. "Christians must still obey the law."
    c. "Go ahead, sin boldly, grace will abound."
    d. "Love covers a multitude of sins."

84. "For as often as you eat this bread and drink the cup, you proclaim the LORD's death until he comes." From which letter does this quotation come?
    a. Romans
    b. 1 Corinthians
    c. Ephesians
    d. 1 Timothy

85. What is the issue that prompts the gathering described in Acts 15?
    a. the debate over circumcision and salvation
    b. the rejection of Jewish law by Gentiles
    c. the replacement of Judas
    d. the way to approach synagogues

86. Which letter contains the following quotation: "Rejoice in the LORD always; again I will say, Rejoice"?
    a. Romans
    b. 2 Corinthians
    c. Ephesians
    d. Philippians

87. Which letter contains this quotation: "So faith, hope, love abide, these three: but the greatest of these is love"?
    a. 1 Corinthians
    b. Ephesians
    c. Philippians
    d. Colossians

88. In Romans, why did Paul say that he was not ashamed of the gospel?
    a. because it came from the risen Lord
    b. because it is the power of God for salvation
    c. because he had Roman citizenship
    d. because he was trained under Gamaliel

89. Who was the first Christian martyr?
    a. Ananias
    b. Paul
    c. Peter
    d. Stephen

90. In 2 Corinthians, what words conclude the following sentence: "If any one is in Christ, he is . . ."?
    a. a child of God
    b. a fellow heir with Christ
    c. a friend of God
    d. a new creation

91. In the first chapter of Acts, what words complete Jesus' commission to the apostles: "But you shall receive power when the Holy Spirit has come upon you; and . . ."
    a. lo, I am with you always, to the close of the age
    b. peace I leave with you; my peace I give to you

c. this is my commandment, that you love one another as I have loved you

d. you shall be my witnesses in Jerusalem and in all Judea and Samaria and to the end of the earth

92. In 2 Timothy, we are told that "all scripture is inspired by God" and that it is profitable for what?
   a. praying
   b. preaching
   c. teaching
   d. worship

93. Where were the disciples called Christians for the first time?
   a. Antioch
   b. Caesarea
   c. Damascus
   d. Jerusalem

Rest of the New Testament

94. What book contains the following quotation: " 'The very stone which the builders rejected has become the head of the corner,' and 'A stone that will make men stumble, a rock that will make them fall' "?
   a. 1 Timothy
   b. James
   c. 1 Peter
   d. Jude

95. Why does the author of Hebrews find Melchizedek to be so important?
   a. As a Gentile, he represents the mission to the Gentiles.
   b. Like Jesus, he suffered for the sins of others.
   c. He is a type of Jesus' priestly work.
   d. He is one of the Old Testament people who was raised from the dead.

96. In one New Testament book, a forest set ablaze by a small fire and the rudder of a ship occur as images for which of the following?
   a. the emotions
   b. the heart
   c. the mind
   d. the tongue

97. What words complete this statement about Christ in the book of Hebrews: "For because he himself has suffered and been tempted . . ."?
   a. he is able to help those who are tempted
   b. he is seated at the right hand of God
   c. he was raised in glory
   d. he was triumphant over sin and death

98. What book contains the following quotation: "Beloved, do not be surprised at the fiery ordeal which comes upon you to prove you"?
   a. Titus
   b. Hebrews
   c. 1 Peter
   d. Jude

99. According to the book of Hebrews, what must one have in order to please God?
   a. deeds
   b. faith
   c. hope
   d. love

100. Which epistle contains the following quotation: ". . . show me your faith apart from your work and I by my works will show you my faith"?
   a. 2 Timothy
   b. Titus
   c. Philemon
   d. James

BIBLE CONTENT EXAM: 1992
Answer Sheet

Pentateuch

1. d. Exodus 32:7–8
2. c. Leviticus 17:14
3. a. Exodus 28:1
4. d. Genesis 35:22
5. d. Exodus 3:5, 7, 13; 20:3
6. c. Genesis 3:2–4
7. c. Exodus 20:2–17; Deuteronomy 5:6–21
8. b. Exodus 18:1
9. d. Exodus 20:18
10. d. Numbers 27:16–18
11. a. Numbers 12:9–10
12. b. Genesis 4:9
13. a. Genesis 9:14
14. c. Exodus 20:3
15. a. Numbers 14:33
16. a. Exodus 33:3
17. c. Genesis 17:11

Historical Books

18. b. Joshua 2:1
19. d. 1 Kings 3:24–25
20. c. Joshua 6:4
21. b. Judges 17:6; 21:25
22. a. 1 Kings 18:17–19
23. a. Judges 4:4
24. d. 1 Kings 8:27
25. a. Ruth 4:17, 21–22
26. b. 1 Kings 21:7
27. d. Judges 13:5, 24
28. a. Joshua 2:21
29. c. 2 Kings 22:8; 2 Chronicles 34:14

Prophets

30. c. Daniel 1:1–16
31. a. Jeremiah 31:33
32. b. Ezekiel 1:1
33. a. Isaiah 9:6
34. b. Ezekiel 37
35. c. Daniel 2:25
36. d. Hosea 1:2ff.
37. a. Jeremiah 1:4

38. d. Jonah 3:4
39. a. Jeremiah 20:7
40. c. Nehemiah 2:8
41. a. Ezekiel 2:1, 3
42. d. Jonah 1:12–15
43. a. Isaiah 6:8
44. d. Micah 6:8
45. b. Ezekiel 3:1
46. a. Joel 2:28
47. b. Jeremiah 37:15, 21; 38:13

Psalms and Wisdom Literature

48. d. Proverbs 15:1
49. b. Proverbs 22:1
50. a. Job 1:6
51. b. Proverbs 22:6
52. b. Psalms 103:11
53. a. Psalms 19:14
54. c. Ecclesiastes 3:1–9
55. b. Job 2:5
56. c. Proverbs 9:10
57. a. Psalms 46:1

Synoptic Gospels

58. a. Mark 1:19
59. c. Luke 4:29
60. d. Luke 17:32
61. d. Mark 1:9
62. c. Luke 2:25–32
63. a. Mark 1:14
64. a. Matthew 1:23
65. d. Mark 5:28
66. c. Mark 14:32
67. d. Matthew 3:13–14; Mark 1:9–13; Luke 3:21–22, 4:11–13
68. a. Matthew 22:39
69. c. Mark 10:45
70. a. Matthew 16:18

Johannine Writings

71. c. John 1:6–8
72. d. 1 John 4:7–11
73. d. Revelation 2—3; 5:6–14; 6:2–8; 12:1
74. c. John 11:3
75. d. Revelation 1:8
76. a. John 1:29

Acts and Pauline Writings

77. a. Acts 2:1–42
78. a. Acts 5:1–11
79. a. Romans 3:23
80. c. Acts 8:27
81. d. Acts 9:1–4
82. b. Galatians 5:6
83. a. Romans 6:2
84. b. 1 Corinthians 11:26
85. a. Acts 15:1–2
86. d. Philippians 4:4
87. a. 1 Corinthians 13:13
88. b. Romans 1:16
89. d. Acts 7:54–60
90. d. 2 Corinthians 5:17
91. d. Acts 1:8
92. c. 2 Timothy 3:16
93. a. Acts 11:26

Rest of the New Testament

94. c. 1 Peter 2:7, 8
95. c. Hebrews 6:20; 7:15
96. d. James 3:4–6
97. a. Hebrews 2:18
98. c. 1 Peter 4:12
99. b. Hebrews 11:6
100. d. James 2:18

BIBLE CONTENT EXAM: 1993

Pentateuch

1. Who was made a leper for her insubordination, but was quickly healed?
   a. Bathsheba
   b. Jezebel
   c. Miriam
   d. Vashti

2. Who was the diviner hired by the king of Moab to curse Israel?
   a. Abiram
   b. Balaam
   c. Dathan
   d. Korah

3. Leviticus 16 speaks of a goat which "shall bear on itself all their inequities to a barren region." Of what ceremony is this goat a part?
   a. daily sin offerings
   b. Day of Atonement
   c. Passover
   d. ritual purification of priests

4. What did circumcision signify, according to the book of Genesis?
   a. that God would never destroy the earth again by flood
   b. the birth of Ishmael
   c. the covenant God made with Abraham and his descendants
   d. the memory of taking Isaac to Mount Moriah

5. In Leviticus, the priestly line is established with the consecration of whom?
   a. Aaron
   b. Eli
   c. Moses
   d. Zadok

6. Whom did Isaac marry?
   a. Leah
   b. Rachel
   c. Rebekah
   d. Tamar

7. What is the name of Moses' brother, who went with Moses to Pharaoh?
   a. Aaron
   b. Caleb
   c. Jethro
   d. Joshua

8. In the days of Noah, why was the Lord grieved in heart and sorry that he had made humankind on the earth?
   a. Cain slew Abel.
   b. God foresaw the building of the tower of Babel.
   c. Noah's children uncovered his nakedness.
   d. The wickedness of humankind was great and the inclination of their hearts was evil.

9. What is the tenth and last plague that struck the land of Egypt before the exodus of the Hebrews?
   a. the death of the first born son in all Egyptian homes
   b. The land had darkness for three days.
   c. The land was full of flies.
   d. The Nile was turned to blood.

10. Abraham was called by God to go out of what place?
   a. Arabia
   b. Canaan
   c. Egypt
   d. Haran

11. Which of the following is not in the Ten Commandments?
   a. "Remember the Sabbath day, to keep it holy."

b. "You shall be holy, for I the LORD your God am holy."

c. "You shall not commit adultery."

d. "You shall not steal."

12. Whom did Jacob cheat out of his birthright?

a. Esau

b. Isaac

c. Ishmael

d. Joseph

13. Which book contains an account of Moses' death and burial?

a. Exodus

b. Leviticus

c. Numbers

d. Deuteronomy

14. What did the mission of the twelve spies accomplish?

a. It caused Miriam to sing a song of victory to the Lord.

b. It caused the rod of Aaron to sprout forth buds and bear ripe almonds.

c. It incited Moses to strike a rock twice so that water came forth.

d. It resulted in Israel remaining in the wilderness for forty years.

15. Where was Aaron required to sprinkle blood on the Day of Atonement?

a. on every Israelite who confessed sin

b. on his sons, who represented the people of Israel

c. on the mercy seat (the covering of the ark of the covenant)

d. on the scapegoat sent out into the wilderness

16. What was the name of Abraham's relative who lived in Sodom?

a. Ammon

b. Hagar

c. Keturah

d. Lot

17. Along with the manna, what meat did God provide for the Israelites during the wilderness wandering?

a. goat

b. lamb

c. pork

d. quail

Historical Books

18. Who called Samuel by name in the middle of the night?

a. Eli

b. Elkanah

c. Hannah

d. the Lord

19. Who was spared in the destruction of Jericho?

a. Dinah

b. Lot and his family

c. Rahab and her household

d. Tamar

20. The duties of a "next of kin" figure strongly in what book?

a. Judges

b. Ruth

c. 1 Kings

d. Esther

21. "Then the Israelites did what was evil in the sight of the LORD and worshiped the Baals; and they abandoned the LORD, the God of their ancestors." This comment is typical of what book?

a. Joshua

b. Judges

c. 1 Samuel

d. 2 Samuel

22. To whom did God say, "My servant Moses is dead. Now proceed to cross the Jordan, you and all this people, into the land that I am giving to them, to the Israelites"?
    a. Aaron
    b. Gideon
    c. Joshua
    d. Samson

23. Who was the prophet who promised that David would never lack an heir to sit upon the throne in Jerusalem?
    a. Ahijah
    b. Deborah
    c. Elijah
    d. Nathan

24. Which of the judges refused to be elected king?
    a. Deborah
    b. Ehud
    c. Gideon
    d. Samson

25. What did Nathan say would be the consequences of David's sin with Bathsheba?
    a. broken treaties with neighboring allies
    b. his army being unprepared
    c. tolerating idols
    d. trouble within his own household

26. Who led three hundred men with trumpets, empty jars, and torches against Midian?
    a. Deborah
    b. Ehud
    c. Gideon
    d. Jephthah

27. Which book records Israel's crossing the Jordan to take possession of the land?
    a. Joshua

b. Judges
c. 1 Samuel
d. 2 Samuel

28. Who directed a battle fought by certain tribes against the Canaanites?
    a. Deborah
    b. Jael
    c. Miriam
    d. Ruth

29. Who anointed Saul king?
    a. Jonathan
    b. the judges of Israel
    c. the Levites
    d. Samuel

Prophets

30. Who was the Canaanite army commander defeated by Deborah and Barak at the river Kishon?
    a. Anak
    b. Cushan
    c. Ehud
    d. Sisera

31. Whose prophecy contains God's instructions about how the prophet is to name his children?
    a. Ezekiel
    b. Hosea
    c. Amos
    d. Micah

32. "Then the eyes of the blind shall be opened, and the ears of the deaf unstopped" is found in which of the following?
    a. Isaiah
    b. Lamentations
    c. Daniel
    d. Amos

33. In what book is the vision of a new covenant to be written on the hearts of God's people found?
    a. Jeremiah
    b. Hosea

c. Amos
d. Micah

34. Which book opens with these words: "How lonely sits the city that once was full of people! How like a widow has she become, she that was great among the nations! She that was a princess among the provinces has become a vassal"?
a. Nehemiah
b. Jeremiah
c. Lamentations
d. Ezekiel

35. Regarding whom was the following said: "I have found among the exiles from Judah a man who can tell the king the interpretation"?
a. Isaiah
b. Jeremiah
c. Ezekiel
d. Daniel

36. "Thus says the LORD of hosts: So will I break this people and this city, as one breaks a potter's vessel, so that it can never be mended" is found in which of the following?
a. Jeremiah
b. Ezekiel
c. Hosea
d. Amos

37. When the sailors cast lots to determine who had caused their calamity, what did they do to Jonah?
a. They arrested him.
b. They put him in chains.
c. They put him in the hold of the ship.
d. They threw him overboard.

38. Which prophet describes this sign: "Look, the young woman . . . shall bear a son, and shall name him Immanuel"?
a. Isaiah

b. Jeremiah
c. Micah
d. Malachi

39. Which prophet addressed most of his oracles to Israel, although he was from Judah?
a. Hosea
b. Amos
c. Obadiah
d. Malachi

40. Which book contains the following quotation: "But he was wounded for our transgressions, crushed for our iniquities; upon him was the punishment that made us whole, and with his bruises we are healed"?
a. Isaiah
b. Jeremiah
c. Ezekiel
d. Daniel

41. "Woe is me, my mother, that you ever bore me, a man of strife and contention to the whole land" is most characteristic of which prophetic book?
a. Jeremiah
b. Ezekiel
c. Hosea
d. Amos

42. Which prophet was commanded, "O mortal, eat what is offered to you; eat this scroll, and go, speak to the house of Israel"?
a. Jeremiah
b. Ezekiel
c. Jonah
d. Micah

43. Why was Daniel cast into the den of lions?
a. He asked to return to Jerusalem.
b. He ate the forbidden meat.

c. He insisted on praying to his God.

d. He prophesied the destruction of the empire.

44. Which prophet said, "Truly I do not know how to speak, for I am only a boy"?
   a. Isaiah
   b. Jeremiah
   c. Ezekiel
   d. Amos

45. According to Ezekiel 1:1, when did Ezekiel's visions occur?
   a. before the Babylonian invasion
   b. during the Babylonian exile
   c. immediately following the fall of Samaria and the Northern Kingdom
   d. shortly after Solomon's death, when the kingdom was divided

46. What was the name of Jeremiah's scribe?
   a. Balaam
   b. Barnabas
   c. Baruch
   d. Benjamin

47. Which book contains many passages concerning a "servant of the LORD"?
   a. Isaiah
   b. Lamentations
   c. Ezekiel
   d. Amos

Psalms and Wisdom Literature

48. Which book contains the following quotation: "Where were you when I laid the foundation of the earth"?
   a. Job
   b. Proverbs
   c. Ecclesiastes
   d. Song of Solomon

49. Which book asks, "A capable wife who can find?"
   a. Job
   b. Psalms
   c. Proverbs
   d. Ecclesiastes

50. The psalm often used as an assurance of pardon, "He does not deal with us according to our sins, nor requite us according to our iniquities," also includes which line?
   a. "For as the heavens are high above the earth, so great is his steadfast love toward those who fear him."
   b. "Hear my cry, O God, listen to my prayer; from the end of the earth I call to thee."
   c. "May God be gracious to us and bless us, and make his face to shine upon us."
   d. "O LORD, open thou my lips, and my mouth shall show forth thy praise."

51. Which of these statements is from Job?
   a. "A time to kill and a time to heal."
   b. "Avert the evil design of Haman."
   c. "Curse God, and die."
   d. "The LORD will keep you from all evil."

52. In which book is the following quotation: "The LORD is my rock, my fortress, and my deliverer, my God, my rock in whom I take refuge"?
   a. Job
   b. Psalms
   c. Proverbs
   d. Song of Solomon

53. Where does the following quotation occur: "A wise child makes a glad father, but a foolish child is a mother's grief"?
    a. Job
    b. Psalms
    c. Proverbs
    d. Ecclesiastes

54. In which book is the bride referred to as a "rose of Sharon, a lily of the valleys"?
    a. Job
    b. Proverbs
    c. Song of Solomon
    d. Hosea

55. In which book do we find the directive to praise God with music and dance?
    a. Ruth
    b. Psalms
    c. Proverbs
    d. Song of Solomon

56. Which book contains the following statement: "A human mind plans the way, but the LORD directs the steps"?
    a. Job
    b. Psalms
    c. Proverbs
    d. Ecclesiastes

57. Where does this quotation appear: "Naked I came from my mother's womb, and naked I shall return there; the LORD gave, and the LORD has taken away; blessed be the name of the LORD"?
    a. Job
    b. Psalms
    c. Proverbs
    d. Song of Solomon

Gospels

58. To whom did Jesus address this statement: "The Spirit of the LORD is upon me"?
    a. inner circle of disciples
    b. John the Baptist
    c. synagogue audience
    d. the Sanhedrin

59. Which of the following said, "My God, my God, why have you forsaken me?"
    a. Jesus
    b. John the Baptist
    c. Judas Iscariot
    d. Stephen

60. Which of the following asked to be seated at the right and left hand of Jesus in his glory?
    a. James and John
    b. Matthew and Judas
    c. Peter and Andrew
    d. Philip and Thomas

61. Which of the following correctly completes Jesus' saying: "No one who puts a hand to the plow and looks back . . ."?
    a. is fit for the kingdom of God
    b. shall be called a prophet of the Most High
    c. shall be exalted in heaven
    d. shall inherit the earth

62. Which of the following went to the tomb on Easter morning to anoint the body of Jesus?
    a. Cleopas
    b. John Mark
    c. Mary Magdalene
    d. Peter

63. Which of the following is not one of the "I am" sayings of Jesus in the Gospel of John?
    a. the good shepherd
    b. the resurrection and the life
    c. the suffering servant
    d. the true vine

64. Which of the following did not earn his living by fishing?
    a. James
    b. John

c. Matthew
d. Peter

65. What was Thomas's response when Jesus offered to let him touch his hands and side?
   a. "My LORD and my God."
   b. "Our LORD and Savior."
   c. "You are the Christ, the Son of God."
   d. "You are the King of Israel."

66. When Jesus interprets the parable of the sower in Mark, he says that the sower was sowing which of the following?
   a. mustard seed
   b. seeds of kindness
   c. tares among the wheat
   d. the word

67. What was Zacchaeus's profession?
   a. centurion
   b. fisherman
   c. priest
   d. tax collector

68. To whom was Jesus referring when he said, "He is Elijah who is to come"?
   a. John the Baptist
   b. Simeon
   c. Zacchaeus
   d. Zechariah

69. Who helped carry the cross for Jesus on the way to Golgotha?
   a. Bartimaeus
   b. Joseph
   c. a Roman soldier
   d. Simon of Cyrene

70. Which of the following is not a saying of Jesus?
   a. "God helps those who help themselves."
   b. "Prophets are not without honor, except in their home-town, and among their own kin."

c. "The sabbath was made for humankind, not humankind for the sabbath."
   d. "Those who are well have no need of a physician, but those who are sick."

71. To what do the parables of leaven, wheat, and tares; hidden treasure; and the dragnet all refer?
   a. instruction given to the seventy
   b. the end of the world
   c. the kingdom of heaven
   d. the second coming

72. Which words immediately follow this statement from John 20:30–31: "Now Jesus did many other signs in the presence of his disciples, which are not written in this book. But these are written so that you may come . . ."?
   a. to believe that Jesus is the Messiah
   b. to believe that Jesus is the Son of God
   c. to have life in Jesus' name
   d. to know all the signs that Jesus did

73. Which of the following was not one of Jesus' temptations?
   a. "All these I will give you, if you will fall down and worship me."
   b. "Command these stones to become loaves of bread."
   c. "If you are the messiah, walk over the sea of Galilee."
   d. "If you are the Son of God, throw yourself down."

74. In the fourth Gospel, who calls Jesus the Lamb of God?
   a. John the Baptist
   b. Mary Magdalene
   c. Nathaniel
   d. Peter

75. What was the answer given to the scribe's question: "Which commandment is first of all?"
    a. "Do unto others as you would have others do unto you."
    b. "Love one another as I have loved you."
    c. "Seek first his kingdom and his righteousness and all these things shall be yours as well."
    d. "You shall love the LORD your God with all your heart, and with all your soul, and with all your mind, and with all your strength."

76. Which Gospel contains the parable of the Good Samaritan?
    a. Matthew
    b. Mark
    c. Luke
    d. John

Acts and Pauline Writings

77. What did the disciples of Jesus do to replace Judas?
    a. They commissioned Matthew to record the teaching of Jesus in a Gospel.
    b. They decided that the eleven disciples who had then received the Holy Spirit were sufficient.
    c. They elected a man converted on the day of Pentecost.
    d. They elected a man who had been with Jesus throughout his ministry.

78. In which epistle does Paul state his desire to visit Spain?
    a. Romans
    b. 1 Corinthians
    c. Galatians
    d. Philemon

79. What word completes the following quotation: "And it was in _____ that the disciples were first called 'Christians' "?
    a. Antioch
    b. Caesarea
    c. Damascus
    d. Jerusalem

80. Where does Paul preach a sermon about the unknown god?
    a. Antioch
    b. Athens
    c. Lystra
    d. Philippi

81. Which letter contains the following quotation: ". . . and when he had given thanks, he broke it, and said, 'This is my body that is for you. Do this in remembrance of me' "?
    a. 1 Corinthians
    b. 2 Corinthians
    c. Galatians
    d. 1 Thessalonians

82. When Paul was brought to trial, he was able to set Pharisees against Sadducees by raising what issue?
    a. fate versus free will
    b. justification by faith
    c. paying taxes to Caesar
    d. resurrection of the dead

83. "Since all have sinned and fall short of the glory of God, they are justified by his grace as a gift, through the redemption which is in Christ Jesus" is a theme from which of the following?
    a. Paul's letter to Rome
    b. Paul's sermon at Mars Hill
    c. Paul's second letter to Corinth
    d. Peter's sermon at Pentecost

84. According to the second chapter of Acts, the early followers of Jesus received the Holy Spirit during what feast?
    a. Booths
    b. Dedication
    c. Passover
    d. Pentecost

85. Paul's words in 1 Corinthians concerning the excellence of love come in the midst of a discussion concerning what?
    a. marriage
    b. salvation of the Gentiles
    c. spiritual gifts
    d. the resurrection of Christ

86. "Wretched man that I am! Who will rescue me from this body of death?" is a cry from whom?
    a. Paul
    b. Peter
    c. Silas
    d. Titus

87. What was Peter's accusation against Ananias and Sapphira (who sold property while keeping back some of the proceeds)?
    a. They dishonored the name of Jesus.
    b. They lied to God.
    c. They spoke blasphemous words.
    d. They were filled with new wine.

88. To which church did Paul write a letter before ever visiting them?
    a. Athens
    b. Corinth
    c. Philippi
    d. Rome

89. Where does the following quotation appear: "But when the fullness of time had come, God sent forth his Son, born of woman, born under the law, to redeem those who were under the law, so that we might receive adoption as children"?
    a. 1 Corinthians
    b. Galatians
    c. Ephesians
    d. 1 Thessalonians

90. Under intense persecution, Paul says in Philippians that "living is Christ." What, then, is dying?
    a. gain
    b. God
    c. loss
    d. Satan

91. According to the opening chapter of Acts, for how many days did the resurrected God appear to the apostles?
    a. three
    b. twelve
    c. forty
    d. fifty

Rest of the New Testament

92. Why do we love, according to 1 John?
    a. because Christ has forgiven our sins
    b. because God first loved us
    c. because love is the fulfillment of the law
    d. because love never fails

93. To whom is the book of Revelation addressed?
    a. seven churches in Asia
    b. the church in Jerusalem
    c. the church in Rome
    d. the Roman emperor

94. According to the letter of James, what are the elders of the church to do for sick church members?
    a. Ask the minister to visit them.
    b. Ask the whole church to pray for them.
    c. Call a physician.
    d. Pray over them and anoint them with oil.

95. What does 2 Peter say to help Christians understand the delay of the coming of the day of the Lord?
    a. It doesn't really matter whether the Lord comes again or not.
    b. The Lord has already come in the person of the Holy Spirit.
    c. The Lord will surely come soon.
    d. With the Lord one day is like a thousand years, and a thousand years as one day.

96. What will happen to the lukewarm Christians in Laodicea?
    a. One like a Son of Man will spit them out of his mouth.
    b. They will be cast into hell.
    c. They will be rebuked.
    d. They will be warmed up.

97. What does James say stains the whole body and is set on fire by hell?
    a. pride
    b. sexual passion
    c. the love of money
    d. the tongue

98. Which of the following is a central concern in 1 Timothy?
    a. circumcision
    b. eschatology
    c. orphans
    d. widows

99. In which book does this line of argumentation appear: "Perhaps this is the reason he was separated from you for a while, so that you might have him back forever, no longer as a slave but more than a slave, a beloved brother"?
    a. Galatians
    b. 1 Timothy
    c. 2 Timothy
    d. Philemon

100. Which book compares Jesus to Melchizedek?
    a. Hebrews
    b. James
    c. 1 Peter
    d. 2 Peter

BIBLE CONTENT EXAM: 1993
Answer Sheet

Pentateuch

1. c. Deuteronomy 24:9; Numbers 12:10–15
2. b. Numbers 22—24
3. b. Leviticus 16:22
4. c. Genesis 17:9–11
5. a. Leviticus 8:6
6. c. Genesis 24:67
7. a. Exodus 4:14
8. d. Genesis 6:5–6
9. a. Exodus 11:1–13:2
10. d. Genesis 12:4
11. b. Leviticus 19:2
12. a. Genesis 27:1–45
13. d. Deuteronomy 34
14. d. Numbers 14:33
15. c. Leviticus 16:14–15
16. d. Genesis 13:8–13; 19
17. d. Exodus 16:13; Numbers 11:31–32

Historical Books

18. d. 1 Samuel 3:2–14
19. a. Joshua 6:22–25
20. b. Ruth 3:9
21. b. Judges 2:11–12
22. c. Joshua 1:2
23. d. 2 Samuel 7:4, 12–16
24. c. Judges 8:23
25. d. 2 Samuel 12:11
26. c. Judges 7:15–16
27. a. Joshua 3
28. a. Judges 4
29. d. 1 Samuel 9:27–10:1

Prophets

30. d. Judges 4:2, 15
31. b. Hosea 1:2–8
32. a. Isaiah 35:5
33. a. Jeremiah 31:33
34. c. Lamentations 1:1
35. d. Daniel 2:25
36. a. Jeremiah 19:11
37. d. Jonah 1:15
38. a. Isaiah 7:14
39. b. Amos 1:1

40. a. Isiah 53:5
41. a. Jeremiah 15:10
42. b. Ezekiel 3:1
43. c. Daniel 6:11–12
44. b. Jeremiah 1:6
45. b. Ezekiel 1:1
46. c. Jeremiah 36:4
47. a. Isaiah 40—55

Psalms and Wisdom Literature

48. a. Job 38:4
49. c. Proverbs 31:10
50. a. Psalm 103:10–11
51. c. Job 2:9
52. b. Psalm 18:2
53. c. Proverbs 10:1
54. c. Song of Solomon 2:1
55. b. Psalm 33:1–3; 47:1; 149:3; 150:4
56. c. Proverbs 16:9
57. a. Job 1:21

Gospels

58. c. Luke 4:18
59. a. Matthew 27:46
60. a. Mark 10:35–37
61. a. Luke 9:62
62. c. Mark 16:1
63. c. John 15:1–11; 10:1–18; 11:25–26
64. c. Matthew 9:9
65. a. John 20:28
66. d. Mark 4:3–20
67. d. Luke 19:2
68. a. Matthew 11:14
69. d. Matthew 27:32
70. a. Mark 2:17; 2:27; 6:4
71. c. Matthew 13:24–30, 33, 44, 47–50
72. d. John 20:30–31
73. c. Matthew 4:1–10
74. a. John 1:29
75. d. Mark 12:30
76. c. Luke 10:30ff.

Acts and Pauline Writings

77. d. Acts 1:26
78. a. Romans 15:24
79. a. Acts 11:26
80. b. Acts 17:22–23
81. a. 1 Corinthians 11:24
82. d. Acts 23:6–10
83. a. Romans 3:23–24
84. d. Acts 2:1
85. c. 1 Corinthians 12—14
86. a. Romans 7:24
87. b. Acts 5:7
88. d. Romans 1:13
89. b. Galatians 4:4–5
90. a. Philippians 1:21
91. c. Acts 1:3

Rest of the New Testament

92. b. 1 John 4:7–12, 19
93. a. Revelation 1:4
94. d. James 5:14
95. d. 2 Peter 3:8
96. a. Revelation 3:16
97. d. James 3:6
98. d. 1 Timothy 5:3–16
99. d. Philemon 1:15–16
100. a. Hebrews 7:11–17

BIBLE CONTENT EXAM: 1994

Pentateuch

1. Which of the following was *not* a son of Noah?
   a. Ham
   b. Japheth
   c. Seth
   d. Shem

2. Who was Ishmael's mother?
   a. Hagar
   b. Hannah
   c. Rebekkah
   d. Zipporah

3. What happened to Jacob when he wrestled with a man at the river Jabbok?
   a. He dreamed about a ladder.
   b. He escaped from Esau.
   c. He received a new name.
   d. He was circumcised.

4. What was the sign of God's covenant with Noah?
   a. circumcision
   b. a dove
   c. an olive branch
   d. a rainbow

5. What position was assigned to the Levites in the Israelites' camp?
   a. around the tabernacle of the covenant
   b. outside the camp
   c. between Judah and Reuben
   d. dispersed among the other tribes

6. Who was sentenced to be a fugitive and a wanderer for killing his brother?
   a. Abel
   b. Cain
   c. Esau
   d. Lot

7. Who was Moses' successor?
   a. Aaron
   b. Caleb
   c. Eli
   d. Joshua

8. Which of the following was *not* a brother of Joseph?
   a. Ephraim
   b. Levi
   c. Judah
   d. Simeon

9. Which statement accurately describes Melchizedek?
   a. He joined Abraham in a military campaign.
   b. He paid tithes to Abraham.
   c. He was king in Hebron.
   d. He was priest of God Most High.

10. To whom was it said: "Look toward heaven, and count the stars, if you are able to count them. . . . So shall your descendants be"?
    a. Abraham
    b. Jacob
    c. Lot
    d. Noah

11. "Sing to the LORD, for he has triumphed gloriously; horse and rider he has thrown into the sea" is a quotation from which of the following?
    a. Aaron
    b. Balaam
    c. Joshua
    d. Miriam

12. Of which of the following was Jethro a priest?
    a. Bethel
    b. Midian
    c. Moab
    d. Ur of the Chaldees

13. Moses was of which house?
    a. Dan
    b. Judah
    c. Levi
    d. Simeon

14. Which of the following is *not* one of the five prescribed offerings of Leviticus?
    a. burnt offering
    b. cereal offering
    c. love offering
    d. sin offering

15. According to the book of Leviticus, which group is to purify themselves and make sacrifices on certain occasions?
    a. servants
    b. sojourners
    c. soldiers
    d. women

16. Israelite law demanded scrupulous care in the treatment of the blood of slain animals. What reason for this is given in Leviticus?
    a. Blood is holy.
    b. Blood is inedible.
    c. Blood is life.
    d. Blood is the choicest part of the animal.

17. According to Leviticus, what happens to all who curse father or mother?
    a. They should be driven out from the people.
    b. They should be put to death.
    c. They should go to the priests to be purified.
    d. They should offer a sacrifice.

Historical Books

18. When did Hannah sing a song of thanksgiving to God?
    a. after Israel's victory over Midian

b. after the birth of Elkanah
    c. after the birth of Samuel
    d. after the death of Sisera

19. Which of the following was *not* an accomplishment of David?
    a. He became king of Israel.
    b. He brought the ark of the covenant to Jerusalem.
    c. He built the Temple in Jerusalem.
    d. He triumphed over Goliath of the Philistines.

20. What did Elijah do for a widow of Zarephath during a great famine?
    a. He baked her barley cakes.
    b. He caused it to rain.
    c. He helped her return to Israel.
    d. He revived the widow's son.

21. Who were separated from one another by a chariot and horses of fire?
    a. Elijah and Elisha
    b. Elijah and Isaiah
    c. Ezekiel and Zechariah
    d. Moses and Joshua

22. Who said to David, "If I am still alive, show me the faithful love of the LORD; but if I die, never cut off your faithful love from my house"?
    a. Absalom
    b. Jonathan
    c. Naomi
    d. Solomon

23. What evidence showed Samson to be a Nazirite from birth?
    a. He made his home in Israel.
    b. He never cut his hair.
    c. He never left the land of Israel.
    d. He was stronger than anyone else.

24. "No one shall be able to stand against you all the days of your life. As I was with Moses, so I will be with you; I will not fail you or forsake you" was said by God to whom?
    a. Deborah
    b. Gideon
    c. Joshua
    d. Samson

25. In Joshua, Rahab, who saved the spies, bound what to the window?
    a. brass snake
    b. golden ball
    c. crimson cord
    d. trumpet

26. Which enemy of the Hebrews did Samson fight?
    a. Edomites
    b. Gibeonites
    c. Moabites
    d. Philistines

27. Who led a revolt against King David?
    a. Absalom
    b. Jeroboam
    c. Nathan
    d. Saul

28. "If only my LORD were with the prophet who is in Samaria! He would cure him of his leprosy" is found in the story of which of the following?
    a. Ahab
    b. Hezekiah
    c. Naaman
    d. Nathan

29. For what was Jehu remembered in Israel?
    a. He assassinated Jezebel and her offspring.
    b. He called down fire from heaven on Mount Carmel.

    c. He fought against the Babylonians.
    d. He helped Solomon build the Temple.

30. The decree of Cyrus regarding the reconstruction of the Jerusalem Temple may be found in which book?
    a. 1 Kings
    b. 2 Kings
    c. Ezra
    d. Daniel

Prophets

31. Which book contains the following prophecy: "a child has been born for us, a son given to us; authority rests upon his shoulders; and he is named Wonderful Counselor, Mighty God, Everlasting Father, Prince of Peace"?
    a. Amos
    b. Hosea
    c. Isaiah
    d. Zechariah

32. Which prophet is addressed by God as follows: "Before I formed you in the womb I knew you, and before you were born I consecrated you; I appointed you a prophet to the nations"?
    a. Ezekiel
    b. Hosea
    c. Jeremiah
    d. Joel

33. Which of the following visions is narrated in the book of Ezekiel?
    a. a basket of ripe figs placed at the Temple altar
    b. a valley of dry bones which spring to life when the prophet speaks to them
    c. an angel riding a white horse
    d. locusts swarming over the farmland of Judah

34. Which prophet preached God's judgment against Nineveh?
    a. Amos
    b. Jonah
    c. Obadiah
    d. Zephaniah

35. How does the prophet Micah answer the question: "What does the LORD require of you?"
    a. "I desire steadfast love and not sacrifice, the knowledge of God rather than burnt offerings."
    b. "Let justice roll down like waters and righteousness like an everflowing stream."
    c. "Rend your hearts and not your clothing. Return to the LORD, your God, for he is gracious and merciful."
    d. "To do justice, and to love kindness, and to walk humbly with your God."

36. What foreigners who threatened Jerusalem were the subject of speeches of Isaiah?
    a. Ammonites
    b. Assyrians
    c. Hittites
    d. Medes

37. In what book are the following found: "a shoot shall come out from the stump of Jesse," "the lion shall eat straw," a child "shall play over the hole of the asp"?
    a. Isaiah
    b. Ezekiel
    c. Daniel
    d. Amos

38. Which prophet was in Judah at the time of the fall of Jerusalem?
    a. Amos
    b. Isaiah
    c. Jeremiah
    d. Micah

39. Which book opens with these words: "How lonely sits the city that once was full of people! How like a widow has she become, she that was great among the nations! She that was a princess among the provinces has become a vassal"?
    a. Jeremiah
    b. Lamentations
    c. Ezekiel
    d. Habakkuk

40. Which book contains the following: "He brought me out by the spirit of the LORD, and set me down in the middle of a valley; it was full of bones"?
    a. Isaiah
    b. Lamentations
    c. Ezekiel
    d. Joel

41. Which prophet was commanded, "O mortal, eat what is offered to you; eat this scroll, and go, speak to the house of Israel"?
    a. Isaiah
    b. Ezekiel
    c. Jonah
    d. Micah

42. Regarding whom was the following said: "I have found among the exiles from Judah a man who can tell the king the interpretation"?
    a. Isaiah
    b. Jeremiah
    c. Ezekiel
    d. Daniel

43. Which passage appears in the book of Joel?
    a. "Come now, let us argue it out, says the LORD: though your sins are like scarlet, they shall be like snow."
    b. "Look, the young woman is with child and shall bear a son,

and shall name him Immanuel."

c. "The earth will be full of the knowledge of the LORD, as the waters cover the sea."

d. "Your sons and daughters shall prophesy, your old men shall dream dreams, and your young men shall see visions."

44. This quotation appears in which prophet: "Then the LORD said, 'Name him Lo-ammi, for you are not my people and I am not your God'"?
   a. Amos
   b. Ezekiel
   c. Hosea
   d. Jonah

45. Amos prophesied during the reign of which king of Israel?
   a. David
   b. Jeroboam II (son of Joash)
   c. Manasseh
   d. Solomon

46. "For three transgressions of Israel, and for four, I will not revoke the punishment; because they sell the righteous for silver, and the needy for a pair of sandals" is found in which book?
   a. Ezekiel
   b. Amos
   c. Micah
   d. Haggai

47. In which book do these characteristic lines appear: "Before I formed you in the womb I knew you," "Cursed be the day on which I was born!" "Is there no balm in Gilead?"
   a. Jeremiah
   b. Ezekiel
   c. Hosea
   d. Job

Psalms

48. "Naked I came from my mother's womb, and naked I shall return there; the LORD gave, and the LORD has taken away; blessed be the name of the LORD" appears in which book?
   a. Amos
   b. Job
   c. Joel
   d. Jonah

49. "Better is a dinner of vegetables where love is than a fatted ox and hatred with it" comes from which book?
   a. Ecclesiastes
   b. Lamentations
   c. Proverbs
   d. Psalms

50. Which book warns that adultery leads one "like an ox to the slaughter"?
   a. Ecclesiastes
   b. Lamentations
   c. Proverbs
   d. Song of Songs

51. Where do we learn that "a wise child loves discipline"?
   a. Job
   b. 1 Samuel
   c. Proverbs
   d. Psalms

52. "Better is a dry morsel with quiet than a house full of feasting with strife" appears in which book?
   a. Ecclesiastes
   b. Proverbs
   c. Psalms
   d. Song of Songs/Solomon

53. "I will both lie down and sleep in peace, for you alone, O LORD, make me lie down in safety" appears in which book?
   a. Ecclesiastes

b. Jonah
c. Proverbs
d. Psalms

54. "Let the day perish in which I was born, and the night that said, 'A man-child is conceived.' . . . Why did I not die at birth, come forth from the womb and expire?" is found in which book?
a. Job
b. Psalms
c. Proverbs
d. Ecclesiastes

55. With what do the last five psalms all begin?
a. "I call upon Thee, O LORD."
b. "I cry with my voice to the LORD."
c. "I will extol thee, my God and King."
d. "Praise the LORD."

56. "My child, keep your father's commandment, and do not forsake your mother's teaching" is found in which of the following?
a. Job
b. Proverbs
c. Ecclesiastes
d. Song of Solomon

57. In which book does the following appear: "What do people gain from all the toil at which they toil under the sun?"
a. Job
b. Psalms
c. Proverbs
d. Ecclesiastes

Gospels

58. According to Matthew 3, while John baptizes with water, with what will the one coming after him baptize?
a. the Holy Spirit and a sword
b. the Holy Spirit and fire

c. the Holy Spirit and the love of the Father
d. the Holy Spirit and truth

59. In his teaching on the mountain in Matthew 5, which of the following does Jesus say about the law?
a. As Jesus increases, the law will decrease.
b. He has come to abolish it.
c. Not a letter, not a stroke will pass from the law until all is accomplished.
d. The law applies only to the scribes and Pharisees.

60. In Matthew 12, what does Jesus say about the Son of Man and the Sabbath?
a. The Sabbath will outlast the Son of Man.
b. The Sabbath will pass away with the coming of the Son of Man.
c. The Son of Man is lord of the Sabbath.
d. The Son of Man observes all the laws of the Sabbath.

61. In misunderstanding Jesus' call to God from the cross, to whom did the bystanders think that he called?
a. Elijah
b. his mother
c. Jeremiah
d. Mary Magdalene

62. Instead of unclean hands, what does Jesus say defiles a person?
a. a person's lack of faith
b. a person's parents
c. demons
d. that which comes out of a person

63. Who appeared with Jesus when he was transfigured on a high mountain?
a. Elijah and John the Baptist

b. Moses and David
c. Moses and Elijah
d. Peter and Andrew

64. At the wedding at Cana, who remarked on the quality of the wine?
a. Jesus' mother
b. other wedding guests
c. the chief steward
d. the disciples

65. Who asked, "How can a man be born when he is old? Can he enter a second time into his mother's womb and be born?"
a. Nathanael
b. Nicodemus
c. Philip
d. Thomas

66. In John's Gospel, who said, "You will never wash my feet"?
a. Judas
b. Peter
c. Philip
d. Thomas

67. To whom did Jesus say, "You are right in saying, 'I have no husband'; for you have had five husbands, and the one you have now is not your husband"?
a. a Samaritan woman
b. a woman of Nazareth
c. Mary, called Magdalene
d. Salome

68. To whom does one of the slaves of the high priest ask, "Did I not see you in the garden with him?"
a. Joseph of Arimathea
b. Judas
c. Peter
d. Thomas

69. Who said, "He must increase, but I must decrease"?
a. Andrew
b. John the Baptist

c. Peter
d. Pilate

70. Who said, "Come and see a man who told me everything I have ever done! He cannot be the Messiah, can he?"
a. a Samaritan woman
b. Mary Magdalene
c. Nathanael
d. Nicodemus

71. In John's Gospel, who asked, "Why was the perfume not sold for three hundred denarii and the money given to the poor?"
a. Judas Iscariot
b. Martha
c. Nathanael
d. Philip

72. Rather than naming him after his father, what did Elizabeth and Zechariah name their son?
a. Andrew
b. John
c. Levi
d. Peter

73. Who climbed a tree in order to see Jesus?
a. Bartimaeus
b. Mary
c. Matthew
d. Zacchaeus

74. Which of these statements is found in the first chapter of Matthew?
a. "Look, the virgin shall conceive and bear a son."
b. "Glory to God in the highest."
c. "We had hoped that he was the one to redeem Israel."
d. "You are the Christ."

75. Who said: "Unless I see the mark of the nails in his hands . . . I will not believe"?
a. Joseph of Arimathea

b. Mary Magdalene
c. Nathanael
d. Thomas

Acts and Pauline Writings

76. When Peter concluded his sermon on the day of Pentecost, what did he invite his hearers to do?
   a. believe in the Lord Jesus Christ and be saved
   b. confess their sins and join the church
   c. repent and be baptized in the name of Jesus Christ
   d. treat each other justly and share their possessions

77. In what context did Paul quote from Greek poets?
   a. his defense before the emperor
   b. his sermon in Antioch of Pisidia
   c. his sermon in front of the Areopagus in Athens
   d. his trial before the proconsul Gallio

78. In what letter does Paul say that "the greatest of these is love"?
   a. Galatians
   b. 1 Corinthians
   c. Romans
   d. 2 Corinthians

79. According to Ephesians, how should husbands love their wives?
   a. as Christ loves the church
   b. as their wives love them
   c. by giving them clothing without spot or wrinkle
   d. by treating them fairly

80. Where was Paul when he wrote to the church in Philippi?
   a. at sea
   b. in prison

c. shipwrecked
d. visiting Aquila and Priscilla

81. What is the conclusion of this retrospective view of Paul's career: "I have fought the good fight . . ."
   a. and Christ has given me the victory
   b. and my strength is made perfect in weakness
   c. I have finished the race, I have kept the faith
   d. my head is bloody but unbowed

82. What word completes the following quotation: "And it was in _____ that the disciples were first called 'Christians' "?
   a. Antioch
   b. Caesarea
   c. Damascus
   d. Jerusalem

83. When the residents of Lystra thought Barnabas was Zeus and Paul was Hermes, what did Barnabas and Paul do?
   a. exhorted the local magistrate to calm the crowd
   b. left the city immediately
   c. refused to acknowledge they understood the local tongue
   d. tore their clothes and delivered a speech

84. In the book of Acts, who was accused of speaking blasphemous words against Moses and God, defended himself with a speech making extensive use of the Old Testament, and was stoned?
   a. Barnabas
   b. Paul
   c. Philip
   d. Stephen

85. For the sake of which church did Paul collect offerings?
   a. Athens

b. Caesarea
c. Ephesus
d. Jerusalem

86. How does Paul answer the question, "Are we to continue in sin that grace may abound?"
    a. By no means. How can we who died to sin still live in it?
    b. Christians must still obey the law.
    c. Go ahead, sin boldly, grace will abound.
    d. Love covers a multitude of sins.

87. To which church did Paul write: ". . . I would rather speak five words with my mind, in order to instruct others also, than ten thousand words in a tongue"?
    a. Corinth
    b. Ephesus
    c. Galatia
    d. Jerusalem

88. Paul's recommendation to the unmarried is found in which of the following?
    a. Romans
    b. 1 Corinthians
    c. Galatians
    d. Philemon

89. When Paul wrote, "My grace is sufficient for you, for power is made perfect in weakness," to what was he referring?
    a. a quotation from the Gospels
    b. a quotation from the Old Testament
    c. what he had learned from the Lord about his thorn in the flesh
    d. what he had learned from the Lord about the church

90. "For by grace you have been saved through faith, and this is not your own doing; it is the gift of God—not the result of works, so that no one may boast" occurs in which book?
    a. Ephesians
    b. Colossians
    c. Titus
    d. Philemon

Rest of the New Testament

91. According to Hebrews, why is Jesus able to sympathize with our weakness?
    a. because he has been tested as we are
    b. because he was poor as some of us are
    c. because he was rejected as we are
    d. because he understands us

92. According to Hebrews, why is Jesus worthy of more glory than Moses?
    a. because he was God's messenger
    b. because he was God's prophet
    c. because he was God's servant
    d. because he was God's son

93. According to Hebrews, which of the following is "the same yesterday and today and forever"?
    a. Jesus Christ
    b. kingdom of God
    c. new covenant
    d. the law of God

94. Where does the following quotation appear: "For just as the body without the spirit is dead, so faith without works is also dead"?
    a. Hebrews
    b. James

c. Jude

d. 1 Peter

95. Where does the following quotation appear: "Endure trials for the sake of discipline. God is treating you as children; for what child is there whom a parent does not discipline?"

a. Hebrews

b. James

c. 1 Peter

d. 2 Peter

96. According to the letter of James, what is the one thing that no one can tame?

a. ambition

b. anger

c. lust

d. the tongue

97. According to 1 Peter, what is the appropriate response when one suffers as a Christian?

a. to endure

b. to pray

c. to rejoice

d. to thank God

98. Where does the following appear: "Likewise, Sodom and Gomorrah and the surrounding cities, which, in the same manner as they, indulged in sexual immorality and pursued unnatural lust, serve as an example by undergoing a punishment of fire"?

a. Hebrews

b. James

c. Jude

d. 1 John

99. Which of the following quotations appears in Hebrews?

a. "Be hospitable to one another without complaining."

b. "Now faith is the assurance of things hoped for, the conviction of things not seen."

c. "So if anyone is in Christ, there is a new creation . . ."

d. "With the LORD one day is like a thousand years, and a thousand years are like one day."

100. "What good is it, my brothers and sisters, if you say you have faith but do not have works? Can faith save you?" This quotation is from which of the following writings?

a. Galatians

b. Ephesians

c. Hebrews

d. James

BIBLE CONTENT EXAM: 1994
Answer Sheet

Pentateuch

1. c. Genesis 9:18
2. a. Genesis 16:15
3. c. Genesis 32:22–26
4. d. Genesis 9:1–17
5. a. Numbers 1:53
6. b. Genesis 4:8–16
7. d. Numbers 27:12–23
8. a. Genesis 35:22–26
9. d. Genesis 14:18
10. a. Genesis 15:5
11. d. Exodus 15:21
12. b. Exodus 18:1
13. c. Exodus 2:1
14. c. Leviticus 1—4
15. d. Leviticus 12:1–8
16. c. Leviticus 17:14
17. b. Leviticus 20:9

Historical Books

18. c. 1 Samuel 1—2
19. c. 2 Samuel 7:12–13
20. d. 1 Kings 17:17–22
21. a. 2 Kings 2:9–11
22. b. 1 Samuel 20:14
23. b. Judges 16:17
24. c. Joshua 1:5
25. c. Joshua 2:21
26. d. Judges 15:14
27. a. 2 Samuel 15
28. c. 2 Kings 5:3
29. a. 2 Kings 9—10
30. c. Ezra 1:1–4

Prophets

31. c. Isaiah 9:6
32. c. Jeremiah 1:5
33. b. Ezekiel 37
34. b. Jonah 3:1–5
35. d. Micah 6:8

36. b. Isaiah 10:24
37. a. Isaiah 11:1, 7–8
38. c. Jeremiah 39
39. b. Lamentations 1:1
40. c. Ezekiel 37:1
41. b. Ezekiel 3:1
42. d. Daniel 2:25
43. d. Joel 2:28
44. c. Hosea 1:9
45. b. Amos 1:1
46. b. Amos 2:6
47. a. Jeremiah 1:5; 8:22; 20:14

Psalms and Wisdom Literature

48. b. Job 1:21
49. c. Proverbs 15:17
50. c. Proverbs 7:22
51. c. Proverbs 13:1
52. b. Proverbs 17:1
53. d. Psalms 4:8
54. a. Job 3:3, 11
55. d. Psalms 146—150
56. b. Proverbs 6:20
57. d. Ecclesiastes 1:3

Gospels

58. b. Matthew 3:11
59. c. Matthew 5:18
60. c. Matthew 12:8
61. a. Matthew 27:47
62. d. Mark 7:15
63. c. Mark 9:4
64. c. John 2:9–10
65. b. John 3:4
66. b. John 13:8
67. a. John 4:17–18
68. c. John 18:26
69. b. John 3:30

70. a. John 4:29
71. a. John 12:5
72. b. Luke 1:59–60
73. d. Luke 19:3–4
74. a. Matthew 1:23
75. d. John 20:25

Acts and Pauline Writings

76. c. Acts 2:38
77. c. Acts 17:28
78. b. 1 Corinthians 13
79. a. Ephesians 5:25, 29
80. b. Philippians 1:7, 13–14
81. c. 2 Timothy 4:7
82. a. Acts 11:26
83. d. Acts 14:14
84. d. Acts 7
85. d. Romans 15:25–27
86. a. Romans 6:2
87. a. 1 Corinthians 14:19
88. b. 1 Corinthians 7
89. c. 2 Corinthians 12:9
90. a. Ephesians 2:8–9

Rest of the New Testament

91. a. Hebrews 4:15
92. d. Hebrews 3:3–6
93. a. Hebrews 13:8
94. b. James 2:26
95. a. Hebrews 12:7
96. d. James 3:8
97. c. 1 Peter 4:13, 16
98. c. Jude v. 7
99. b. Hebrews 11:1
100. d. James 2:14

BIBLE CONTENT EXAM: 1995

Pentateuch

1. In the book of Genesis, God's promise to Abraham follows most closely on which story?
   a. the creation
   b. the flood
   c. the murder of Abel
   d. the tower of Babel

2. With what were Abraham and David both closely associated?
   a. Hebron
   b. Jericho
   c. Nineveh
   d. Peniel

3. Why did Jacob receive the blessing from Isaac meant for Esau?
   a. because he obeyed Rebekah
   b. because he prepared an acceptable sacrifice
   c. because he was totally honest
   d. because Isaac preferred him over Esau

4. What did Jacob call the place where he took the stone that he had put under his head and set it up for a pillar?
   a. Beersheba
   b. Bethel
   c. Haran
   d. Shechem

5. Who was the spouse of Jacob?
   a. Dinah
   b. Miriam
   c. Rachel
   d. Rebekah

6. "I will not let you go, unless you bless me" was said by whom?
   a. Abraham
   b. Isaac
   c. Jacob
   d. Laban

7. Who said: "Even though you intended to do harm to me, God intended it for good"?
   a. Cain
   b. Jacob
   c. Joseph
   d. Lot

8. The pharaoh's order that the slaves had to provide their own straw for brickmaking was a reaction to what?
   a. Moses' act of murder and his flight
   b. death of his firstborn son
   c. the request to go into the wilderness for a feast day
   d. turning the water into blood

9. The feast celebrating the flight of the Hebrews from Egypt is called what?
   a. Booths
   b. Ingathering
   c. Jubilee
   d. Passover

10. Where was manna first given?
    a. Damascus
    b. Egypt
    c. Jericho
    d. Wilderness of Sin

11. "Three times in the year you shall hold a festival for me." The three feasts are: Weeks (or the harvest of the first fruits), Booths (or the feast of the Ingathering), and which of the following?
    a. Day of Atonement
    b. Hanukkah
    c. Jubilee
    d. Unleavened Bread

12. When Moses delayed coming down from Sinai, what happened?
    a. Aaron made a molten calf.

b. Aaron waited patiently.
c. The people began to leave.
d. The people made a molten calf.

13. To whom were the laws in Leviticus delivered?
a. Aaron
b. Eleazar
c. Joshua
d. Moses

14. With what event are the scapegoat, Aaron, and sin offering connected?
a. Day of Atonement
b. Feast of Harvest
c. Feast of Ingathering
d. Passover

15. "The LORD bless you and keep you; the LORD make his face to shine upon you, and be gracious to you; the LORD lift up his countenance upon you, and give you peace" may be found in which of the following?
a. Genesis
b. Exodus
c. Leviticus
d. Numbers

16. God denied Moses permission to accompany the Israelites into the Promised Land because Moses had done which of the following?
a. allowed the Israelites to intermarry with pagans and to worship foreign gods
b. failed to follow Yahweh's instructions concerning the building of the sanctuary
c. failed to give satisfactory credit to Yahweh for causing water to spring from a rock
d. fathered children who were unfaithful to Yahweh

17. Moses views the Promised Land but is told he will not go there in which of the following books?
a. Exodus
b. Leviticus
c. Numbers
d. Deuteronomy

Historical Books

18. The story of the Israelite defeat of Canaan is narrated in which book?
a. Joshua
b. Judges
c. 1 Samuel
d. 2 Samuel

19. Where did Joshua send two men as spies?
a. Gilgal
b. Jericho
c. Lebanon
d. Shittim

20. According to Joshua 2, what did Rahab do?
a. helped the men of Jericho prepare for war
b. hid Israelite spies
c. hid soldiers for the king
d. warned the city of enemy attack

21. In the time of Joshua, Israel was defeated at Ai because Achan had done which of the following?
a. failed to break his pot at the appointed time
b. had a superior force in chariots
c. mistook the smoke signal and retreated
d. took some of the devoted things after the fall of Jericho

22. Which tribe of Israel received cities within the territories of others?
a. Benjamin

b. Ephraim
c. Judah
d. Levi

23. Why did Joshua gather the tribes of Israel at Shechem?
a. to begin a census
b. to conscript some of the men for the army
c. to establish a religious ritual
d. to make a covenant with them

24. Which individual was Deborah's general?
a. Barak
b. Heber
c. Jael
d. Sisera

25. "The stars fought from heaven, from their courses they fought against Sisera." This famous war song tells of the defeat and death of Sisera who was a commander of which of the following?
a. a Canaanite army during the period of the Judges
b. Absolom's forces in the rebellion against David
c. an Amorite force defeated by Joshua
d. Saul's army, defeated by David

26. What judge—"a Nazirite to God from birth"—would begin to deliver Israel from the hand of the Philistines'?
a. Ehud
b. Gideon
c. Jephthah
d. Samson

27. Who was the first king of the Northern Kingdom (Israel), the one whose sins were said to have been repeated by every king of Israel who followed him?
a. Ahab
b. Hezekiah

c. Jehu
d. Jeroboam

28. Ahab was most closely associated with which group?
a. Babylon
b. Israel
c. Judah
d. Syria

29. "As they continued walking and talking, a chariot of fire and horses of fire separated the two of them" and one of them "ascended in a whirlwind into heaven." Who was carried up into heaven?
a. Daniel
b. Elijah
c. Elisha
d. Enoch

30. What did Saul do to make Samuel turn against him?
a. claimed to be king despite Samuel's opposition
b. failed to destroy the Amalekites completely
c. refused to acknowledge David
d. refused to acknowledge Yahweh

Prophets

31. "Comfort, O comfort my people, says your God. Speak tenderly to Jerusalem" is found in which of the following?
a. Isaiah
b. Jeremiah
c. Hosea
d. Habakkuk

32. Which book contains the following lines: "In the wilderness prepare the way of the LORD"; "He will feed his flock like a shepherd"?
a. Daniel
b. Amos

c. Hosea
d. Isaiah

33. Which book contains the following quotation: "But he was wounded for our transgressions, crushed for our iniquities; upon him was the punishment that made us whole, and by his bruises we are healed"?
a. Isaiah
b. Jeremiah
c. Ezekiel
d. Daniel

34. "Then the LORD put out his hand and touched my mouth; and the LORD said to me, 'Now I have put my words in your mouth. See, today I appoint you over nations and over kingdoms, to pluck up and to pull down, to destroy and to overthrow, to build and to plant.' " Where is this statement found?
a. Jeremiah
b. Hosea
c. Amos
d. Zephaniah

35. In what book does the image of the potter and his clay symbolize God and his people?
a. Jeremiah
b. Daniel
c. Hosea
d. Obadiah

36. Counsel to submit to the yoke of the king of Babylon was given by which of the following?
a. Amos
b. Isaiah
c. Jeremiah
d. Micah

37. What prophet was sitting among the exiles by the river Chebar, during the fifth year of the exile of King Jehoiachin, when he saw visions of God?
a. Ezekiel
b. Haggai
c. Joel
d. Zechariah

38. For an example of the story of the call of a prophet, to which book would one turn?
a. Ezekiel
b. Joel
c. Zechariah
d. Malachi

39. Which book contains the following quotation: "And he said to me, O mortal, stand up on your feet, and I will speak with you. . . . I am sending you to the people of Israel, to a nation of rebels who have rebelled against me"?
a. Ezekiel
b. Daniel
c. Jonah
d. Micah

40. Which prophet refused to eat the food of the Babylonian king while living at the Babylonian court?
a. Jeremiah
b. Ezekiel
c. Daniel
d. Jonah

41. Who was the interpreter of Nebuchadnezzar's dreams?
a. Daniel
b. Ezekiel
c. Joseph
d. Micah

42. Marital infidelity provided a basis for the prophetic message of which of the following?
a. Amos

b. Hosea
c. Joel
d. Micah

43. Which words from the Lord were spoken to Hosea the prophet?
    a. "Seek the LORD while he may be found, call upon him while he is near."
    b. "He said to me, Mortal, can these bones live?"
    c. The Lord said, "Go, take yourself a wife of whoredom and have children of whoredom."
    d. "I take no delight in your solemn assemblies."

44. Which book contains the following: "Then afterward I will pour out my spirit on all flesh; your sons and your daughters shall prophesy, your old men shall dream dreams, and your young men shall see visions"?
    a. Joel
    b. Jonah
    c. Habakkuk
    d. Malachi

45. "I hate, I despise your festivals, and I take no delight in your solemn assemblies. . . . But let justice roll down like waters, and righteousness like an ever-flowing stream." Where does this appear?
    a. Isaiah
    b. Jeremiah
    c. Joel
    d. Amos

46. What was Jonah's message to Ninevah?
    a. a threat of destruction if they did not repent
    b. a warning to flee from the wrath to come

c. an offer of forgiveness if they would repent
d. an announcement that the city will be overthrown

47. Which book contains all of the following: Samaria and Jerusalem will fall, Zion will be restored, and that a Ruler will come from Bethlehem?
    a. Amos
    b. Jonah
    c. Micah
    d. Malachi

Psalms and Wisdom Literature

48. In which book does the following quotation occur: "Shall we receive the good at the hand of God, and not receive the bad?"
    a. Job
    b. Psalms
    c. Proverbs
    d. Ecclesiastes

49. In the final chapter of the book of Job, with whom is God angry?
    a. Job
    b. Job's children
    c. Job's friends
    d. Job's wife

50. How is the following saying, which occurs in Psalms 14 and 53, completed: "Fools say in their hearts, 'There is no . . .' "?
    a. God
    b. justice
    c. mercy
    d. salvation

51. Which of the following completes the quotation from Psalms: "For as the heavens are high above the earth . . ."?
    a. he has not dealt with us according to our sins

b. so great is his steadfast love toward those who fear him

c. so the LORD remembers that we are dust

d. the LORD works vindication and justice for all who are oppressed

52. "Out of the depths I cry to you, O Lord!" is found in which book?
    a. Job
    b. Psalms
    c. Proverbs
    d. Ecclesiastes

53. "By the rivers of Babylon—there we sat down and there we wept" is followed in the biblical text by what line?
    a. I have set my king in Zion.
    b. Sing us one of the songs of Zion.
    c. when we remembered Zion
    d. Why do the nations conspire and the people plot in vain?

54. With what are the last six psalms of the Psalter concerned?
    a. deliverance from evil people
    b. the love of the law
    c. the praise of God
    d. the smiting of Israel's enemies

55. "But again, this also was vanity." This sentiment is characteristic of which book?
    a. Job
    b. Proverbs
    c. Ecclesiastes
    d. Song of Solomon

56. Which of the following completes the quotation from Proverbs: "A good name is to be chosen rather than . . ."?
    a. acclaim of kings
    b. great riches
    c. high position
    d. soundness of body

57. In the book of Proverbs, who is described as "far more precious than jewels"?
    a. a good wife
    b. Lady Wisdom
    c. Solomon's mother
    d. Zion

Gospels

58. Which Gospel or Gospels open with a genealogy?
    a. Matthew
    b. Mark
    c. Luke
    d. Mark and Luke

59. When the angel appeared to Joseph, he told him to name the child Jesus, because:
    a. he is the Lamb of God
    b. he is the Light of the World
    c. he will be called the Son of the Most High
    d. he will save his people from their sins

60. Who asked the question: "Are you the one who is to come, or are we to wait for another?"
    a. Andrew
    b. Herod
    c. John the Baptist
    d. Martha

61. What one sign did Jesus promise the people?
    a. the hungry are fed and the sick healed
    b. the dead are raised
    c. the sign of Jonah
    d. the sign of the cross

62. Which is the only miracle reported in all four Gospels?
    a. feeding the multitudes
    b. healing of blind Bartimaeus
    c. healing of the ten lepers
    d. walking on water

63. "You are Peter, and on this rock I will build my church" is found in which of the following?
    a. Matthew
    b. Mark
    c. Luke
    d. John

64. Who appeared with Moses during the transfiguration of Jesus?
    a. Abraham
    b. Elijah
    c. Elisha
    d. Ezekiel

65. When asked which commandment is greatest, Jesus answered, "You shall love the LORD your God with all your heart, and with all your soul, and with all your mind." What did he say was the second commandment?
    a. "Honor your father and your mother."
    b. "You shall have no other gods before me."
    c. "You shall love your neighbor as yourself."
    d. "You shall not make for yourself a graven image."

66. "Keep awake therefore, for you know neither the day nor the hour" is the conclusion to which parable?
    a. the fig tree
    b. the talents
    c. the ten virgins
    d. the wicked tenants

67. Who said, "Sir, even the dogs under the table eat the children's crumbs"?
    a. Judas
    b. Mary Magdalene
    c. Peter
    d. Syrophoenician woman

68. What was Gethsemane?
    a. a hill where Jesus was crucified
    b. a place where Jesus prayed
    c. a valley where garbage was burned
    d. a village where Jesus borrowed a colt

69. What Gospel reports the young man fleeing from the arrest of Jesus?
    a. Matthew
    b. Mark
    c. Luke
    d. John

70. How does Luke's Gospel begin?
    a. "An account of the genealogy of Jesus the Messiah . . ."
    b. "In the beginning was the Word . . ."
    c. "Since many have undertaken to set down an orderly account of the events that have been fulfilled among us . . ."
    d. "The beginning of the good news of Jesus Christ . . ."

71. Which Gospel contains the parable of the "Good Samaritan"?
    a. Matthew
    b. Mark
    c. Luke
    d. John

72. According to Luke, at which moment did the disciples who journeyed to Emmaus recognize Jesus?
    a. when he broke bread and gave it to them
    b. when he gave them the Holy Spirit
    c. when he opened the scriptures
    d. when he showed them the nail prints in his hands

73. What book contains passages describing the role and function of the Paraclete or Advocate?
    a. Matthew
    b. Mark

c. Luke
d. John

74. Who said, "What is truth?"
    a. Jesus
    b. Peter
    c. Pilate
    d. the rich young man

75. What does the closing verse of John's Gospel declare?
    a. A second book will be written, dealing with the history of the church.
    b. Jesus did so many things, the world itself could not contain the books that would be written.
    c. No one should add to or take away from anything in the book.
    d. Whoever brings back a sinner from wandering will save the sinner's soul from death.

Acts and Pauline Writings

76. Which book is addressed to a man named Theophilus?
    a. Acts
    b. Romans
    c. 1 Corinthians
    d. 1 Thessalonians

77. In the first chapter of Acts, what words complete Jesus' commission to the apostles: "But you will receive power when the Holy Spirit has come upon you; and . . ."?
    a. lo, I am with you always, to the close of the age
    b. peace I leave with you; my peace I give to you
    c. this is my commandment, that you love one another as I have loved you
    d. you will be my witnesses in Jerusalem, in all Judea and Samaria, and to the end of the earth

78. The people gathered in the upper room after Jesus was lifted up into heaven included which of the following?
    a. Barnabas
    b. Mary
    c. Nicodemus
    d. Timothy

79. After the apostles were arrested by the Jerusalem authorities and beaten for refusing to cease teaching in the name of Jesus, the book of Acts tells us: "As they left the council, they rejoiced . . ." for what reason?
    a. that day by day the Lord added to their number
    b. that the Lord gave them power to testify to the gospel
    c. that the Lord had set them free
    d. that they were considered worthy to suffer dishonor for the sake of the name

80. In Romans, why did Paul say that he was not ashamed of the gospel?
    a. because he had Roman citizenship
    b. because he was trained under Gamaliel
    c. because it came from the risen Lord
    d. because it is the power of God for salvation

81. Which statement best summarizes Paul's argument in Romans that there is no difference between Jew and Greek?
    a. they all need milk, not solid food

b. they are the temple of the living God

c. they all have sinned and fall short of the glory of God

d. they have this treasure in earthen vessels

82. In Romans, Paul sets one man, Jesus Christ, who brought the free gift of grace and eternal life, in contrast with what other man?
a. Abraham
b. Adam
c. David
d. Melchizedek

83. Which book says: ". . . has God rejected his people? By no means"?
a. John
b. Romans
c. 2 Corinthians
d. Hebrews

84. Paul's instructions, "If you are hungry, eat at home" pertains to which of the following?
a. conditioning for the trip to Corinth
b. eating of food offered to idols
c. preparation for a Jewish festival
d. the Lord's Supper

85. Which letter contains this quotation: "And now faith, hope, and love abide, these three; and the greatest of these is love"?
a. 1 Corinthians
b. Philippians
c. Colossians
d. 2 Corinthians

86. In 2 Corinthians Paul asserts that Christ was made sin for us so that we might be what?
a. glorified
b. justified

c. reconciled
d. sanctified

87. "For freedom Christ has set us free. Stand firm, therefore, and do not submit again to a yoke of slavery." Where is this found?
a. Romans
b. Corinthians
c. Galatians
d. Colossians

88. Which book contains the following: "Husbands, love your wives, just as Christ loved the church and gave himself up for her"?
a. 2 Corinthians
b. Galatians
c. Ephesians
d. Philippians

89. Which letter contains the following quotation: "Rejoice in the LORD always; again I will say, Rejoice"?
a. Romans
b. 2 Corinthians
c. Ephesians
d. Philippians

90. "Then we who are alive, who are left, will be caught up in the clouds together with them to meet the LORD in the air . . ." occurs in which book?
a. 2 Corinthians
b. Galatians
c. Ephesians
d. 1 Thessalonians

Rest of the New Testament

91. Which words best describe the special message of the book of Hebrews concerning the death of Christ?
a. a ransom to set us free

b. both priest and sacrifice

c. breaking down the dividing wall of hostility

d. suffering servant

92. Which book calls Jesus our faith's pioneer and perfecter?

a. Acts

b. Romans

c. 2 Corinthians

d. Hebrews

93. "If a brother or sister is naked and lacks daily food, and one of you says to them, 'Go in peace; keep warm and eat your fill,' and yet you do not supply their bodily needs, what is the good of that?" is typical of the argument of what book?

a. Hebrews

b. James

c. Jude

d. 1 Peter

94. The tongue is equated with a fire in which of the following?

a. Hebrews

b. James

c. 2 Peter

d. Jude

95. "But you are a chosen race, a royal priesthood, a holy nation, God's own people, in order that you may proclaim the mighty acts of him who called you out of darkness into his marvelous light" occurs in what book?

a. James

b. 1 Peter

c. 1 John

d. Jude

96. "So also our beloved brother Paul wrote to you . . . speaking of this as he does in all his letters. There are some things in them hard to understand" is found in which of the following?

a. James

b. 2 Peter

c. 1 John

d. 2 John

97. "Beloved, we are God's children now; what we will be has not yet been revealed. What we do know is this: when he is revealed, we will be like him, for we will see him as he is." This occurs in which of the following?

a. John

b. 1 John

c. 2 John

d. Revelation

98. "Beloved, let us love one another, because love is from God. . . . Whoever does not love does not know God; for God is love" occurs in which book?

a. James

b. 1 Peter

c. 1 John

d. Revelation

99. " 'I am the Alpha and the Omega' says the LORD God, who is and who was and who is to come, the Almighty." What book contains these words?

a. John

b. 1 John

c. 3 John

d. Revelation

100. Which event occurs earliest in the book of Revelation?

a. giving of seven trumpets

b. opening of the seven seals

c. seven angels with seven plagues

d. vision of Christ with seven messages

BIBLE CONTENT EXAM: 1995
Answer Sheet

Pentateuch

1. d. Genesis 11:1–12:3
2. a. Gen. 13:18; 23:2,19;
   1 Sam. 30:31;
   2 Sam. 2:1, 3, 11
3. a. Genesis 27:6–17
4. b. Genesis 28:18–19
5. c. Genesis 29:28
6. c. Genesis 32:26
7. c. Genesis 50:20
8. c. Exodus 5:1–14
9. d. Exodus 12:11
10. d. Exodus 16:1; 16:31
11. d. Exodus 23:14–16
12. a. Exodus 32:4
13. d. Leviticus 1:1
14. a. Leviticus 16
15. d. Numbers 6:24–26
16. c. Numbers 20:12;
    Deuteronomy
    32:50–51
17. d. Deuteronomy 34:4

Historical Books

18. a. Joshua 1—11
19. b. Joshua 2:1
20. b. Joshua 2:1–7
21. d. Joshua 7:1
22. d. Joshua 21
23. d. Joshua 24:25
24. a. Judges 4:6
25. a. Judges 5:19–20
26. d. Judges 13:5, 24
27. d. 1 Kings 13:33–34;
    15:34; 16:26, 31;
    22:52; 2 Kings
    10:29; 13:2
28. b. 1 Kings 16:29
29. b. 2 Kings 2:11
30. b. 1 Samuel 15:9–11

Prophets

31. a. Isaiah 40:1–2
32. d. Isaiah 40:3, 11
33. a. Isaiah 53:5
34. a. Jeremiah 1:9–10

35. a. Jeremiah 18—19
36. c. Jeremiah 27:11
37. a. Ezekiel 1:1–2
38. a. Ezekiel 1—2
39. a. Ezekiel 2:1, 3
40. c. Daniel 1:1–16
41. a. Daniel 2
42. b. Hosea 1
43. c. Hosea 1:2
44. a. Joel 2:28
45. d. Amos 5:21, 24
46. d. Jonah 3:4
47. c. Micah 1:6; 8–16;
    4:6–13; 5:2

Psalms and Wisdom Literature

48. a. Job 2:10
49. c. Job 42:7
50. a. Psalms 14:1; 53:1
51. b. Psalms 103:11
52. b. Psalms 130:1
53. c. Psalms 137:1
54. c. Psalms 145—150
55. c. Ecclesiastes 2:1
56. b. Proverbs 22:1
57. a. Proverbs 31:10

Gospels

58. a. Matthew 1:1–17
59. d. Matthew 1:21
60. c. Matthew 11:3;
    Luke 7:20
61. c. Matthew 12:39
62. a. Matthew 14:13–21;
    Mark 6:30–44;
    Luke 9:10–17;
    John 6:1–15
63. a. Matthew 16:18
64. b. Matthew 17:3
65. c. Matthew 22:39
66. c. Matthew 25:13
67. d. Mark 7:28
68. b. Mark 14:32
69. b. Mark 14:51–52
70. c. Luke 1:1

71. c. Luke 10:29–37
72. a. Luke 24:30–31
73. d. John 14:16–17, 26;
    15:26; 16:7–11
74. c. John 18:38
75. b. John 21:25

Acts and Pauline Writings

76. a. Acts 1:1
77. d. Acts 1:8
78. b. Acts 1:14
79. d. Acts 5:41
80. d. Romans 1:16
81. c. Romans 3:23
82. b. Romans 5:12–21
83. b. Romans 11:1
84. d. 1 Corinthians
    11:34
85. a. 1 Corinthians
    13:13
86. c. 2 Corinthians
    5:16–21
87. c. Galatians 5:1
88. b. Ephesians 5:25
89. d. Philippians 4:4
90. d. 1 Thessalonians
    4:17

Rest of the New Testament

91. b. Hebrews 2:17;
    4:14–5:10; 7:1–28;
    10:11–18
92. d. Hebrews 12:2
93. b. James 2:15–16
94. b. James 3:6
95. b. 1 Peter 2:9–10
96. b. 2 Peter 3:15–16
97. b. 1 John 3:2
98. c. 1 John 4:7–8
99. d. Revelation 1:8
100. d. Revelation
    1:11–3:22

APPENDIX B: MAPS AND CHARTS

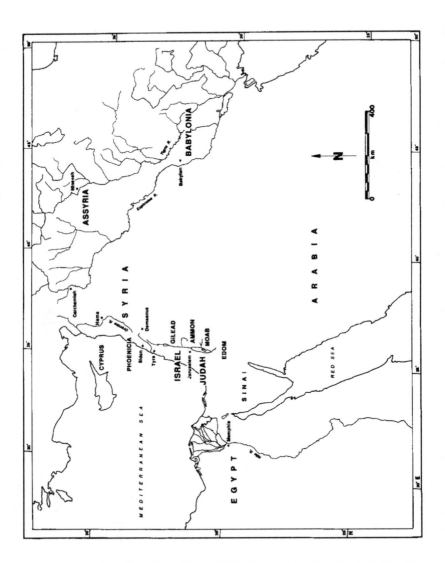

Fig. 1. The ancient Near East. (From Philip King, *Jeremiah: An Archaelogical Companion,* p. 28. Louisville, Ky.: Westminster/John Knox Press, 1993.)

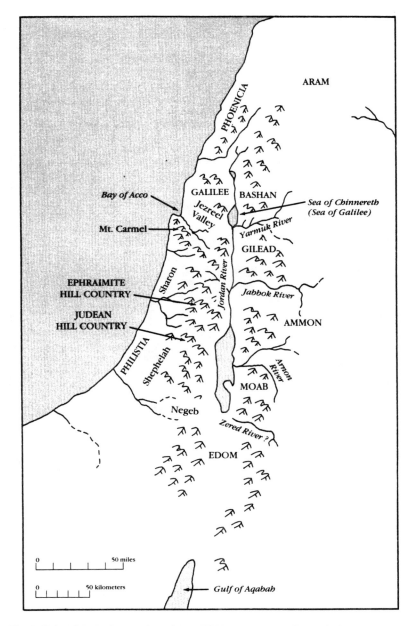

Fig. 2. Palestine during ancient times (3200–332 B.C.E.). (From J. Maxwell Miller and John H. Hayes, *A History of Ancient Israel and Judah*, p. 41. Philadelphia: Westminster Press, 1986.)

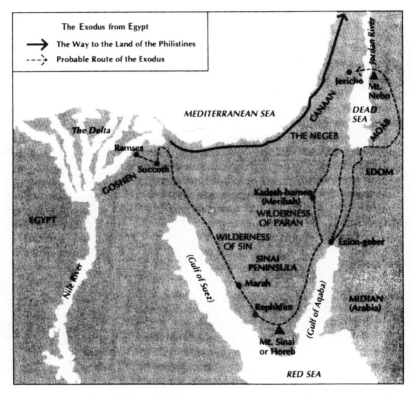

Fig. 3. The exodus and the desert routes. (From Marshall, *A Guide through the Old Testament*, p. 45.)

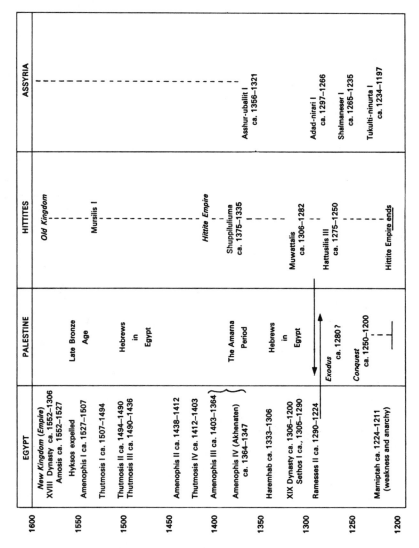

Fig. 4. Chronology of Israel and its neighbors. (From John Bright, *A History of Israel,* 3rd ed., pp. 468–472. Philadelphia: Westminster Press, 1981.) (*Figure continues*)

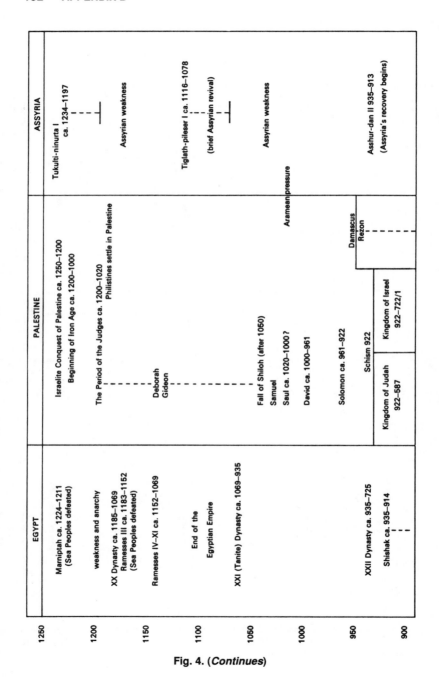

Fig. 4. (*Continues*)

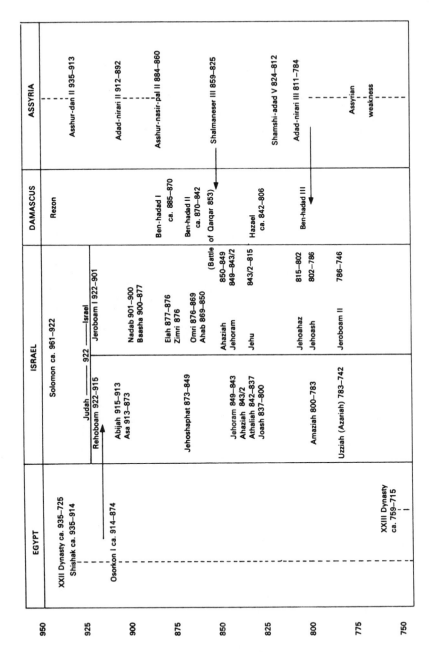

Fig. 4. (*Continues*)

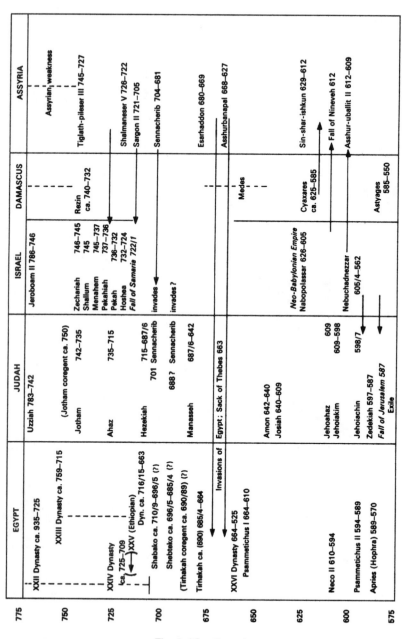

Fig. 4. (*Continues*)

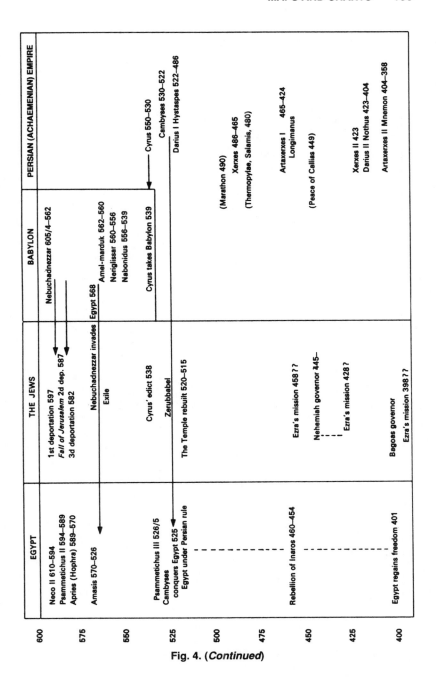

Fig. 4. (*Continued*)

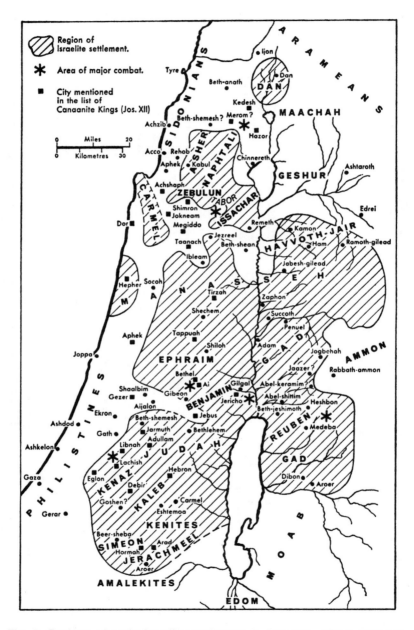

Fig. 5. Regions of early Israelite settlement in Palestine. (From Yohanon Aharoni, *The Land of the Bible: A Historical Geography*, p. 213. Philadelphia: Westminster Press, 1980.)

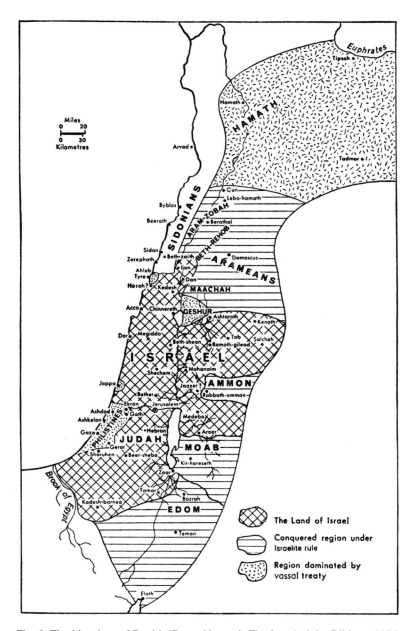

Fig. 6. The kingdom of David. (From Aharoni, *The Land of the Bible*, p. 295.)

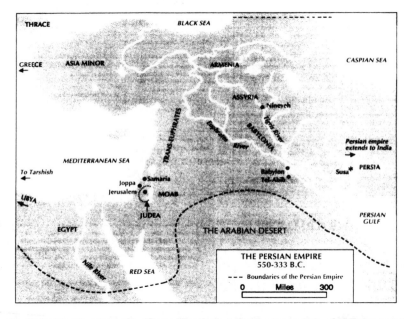

Fig. 7. Judea after the exile. (From Marshall, *A Guide through the Old Testament*, p. 123.)

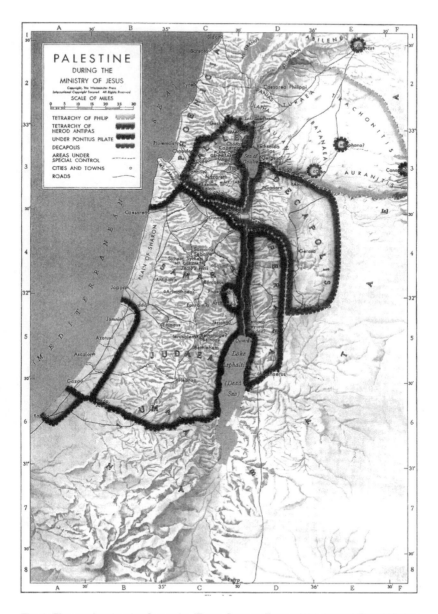

Fig. 8. The setting for the Gospels. (From George Ernest Wright and Floyd Vivian Filson, eds., *The Westminster Historical Atlas to the Bible,* **p. 82. Philadelphia: Westminster Press, 1945.)**

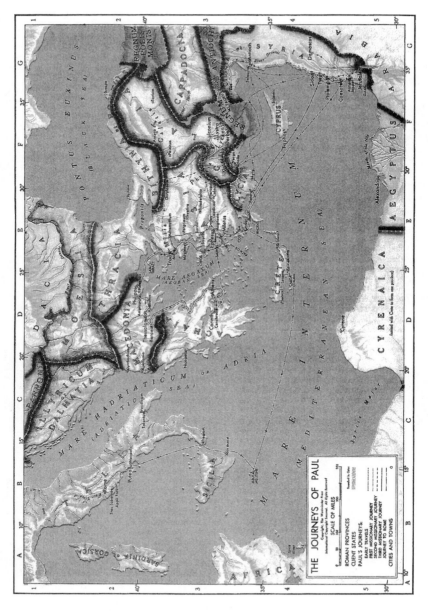

Fig. 9. The setting for Acts. (From Wright and Filson, eds., *The Westminster Historical Atlas to the Bible,* p. 91.)

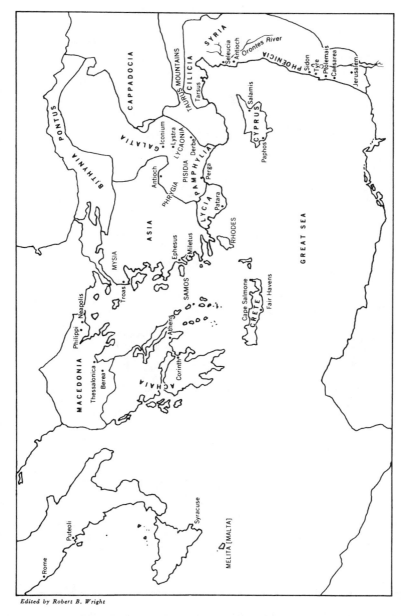

Edited by Robert B. Wright

Fig. 10. The setting for Paul's letters. (From Gehman, *The New Westminster Dictionary*, p. 311.)

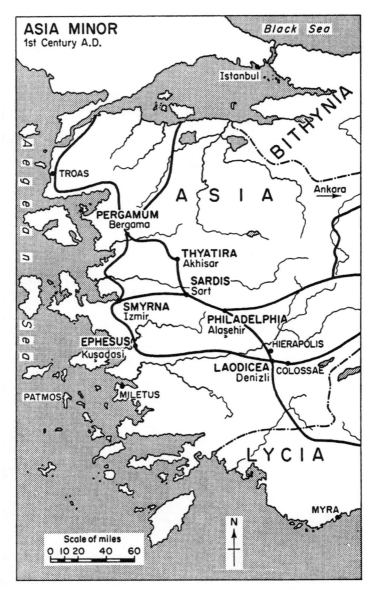

Fig. 11. The setting for Revelation. (From J. P. M. Sweet, *Revelation,* Westminster Pelican Commentary, p. xvi. Philadelphia: Westminster Press, 1979.)

APPENDIX C: SUGGESTED READING LIST

I. Bible Versions

Good News for Modern Man: The New Testament in Today's Version. New York: American Bible Society, 1971.

The Holy Bible: New International Version. Nashville: Holman Bible Publishers, 1986.

The Holy Bible: New Revised Standard Version. New York: Oxford University Press, 1989. *The HarperCollins Study Bible,* based on the *New Revised Standard Version* and published in 1993, is recommended if one is able to purchase just one Bible.

The Jerusalem Bible. Garden City, N.Y.: Doubleday & Co., 1966.

The Living Bible: Paraphrased. Wheaton, Ill.: Tyndale House Publishers, 1971.

The New American Standard Bible. Nashville: Holman Bible Publishers, 1977.

The New English Bible with the Apocrypha. New York: Oxford University Press, 1970.

Phillips, J. B. *The New Testament in Modern English.* London: Geoffrey Bles, 1960.

II. Bible Dictionaries

Achtemeier, Paul J., ed. *Harper's Bible Dictionary.* San Francisco: Harper & Row, 1985.

Bromiley, G. W., ed. *The International Bible Encyclopedia.* 4 vols. Grand Rapids: Wm. B. Eerdmans Publishing Co., 1979.

Buttrick, George A., ed. *The Interpreter's Dictionary of the Bible.* 4 vols. Nashville: Abingdon Press, 1962.

Gehman, Henry Snyder, ed. *The New Westminster Dictionary of the Bible.* Louisville, Ky.: Westminster/John Knox Press, 1970.

Smith, Barbara. *The Westminster Concise Bible Dictionary.* Philadelphia: Westminster Press, 1981.

III. Bible Commentaries

Albright, W. F., and David Noel Freedman, eds. *The Anchor Bible.* Garden City, N.Y.: Doubleday & Co., 1964–1994.

Buttrick, George A., ed. *The Interpreter's Bible.* 12 vols. Nashville: Abingdon Press, 1952–1957.

Gibson, John C. L., and William Barclay, eds. *Daily Study Bible.* 60 vols. Louisville, Ky.: Westminster/John Knox Press, 1975–1986.

Guthrie, Donald, J. A. Motyer, and A. M. Stibbs, eds. *The New Bible Commentary*. 3d ed. Grand Rapids: Wm. B. Eerdmans Publishing Co., 1970.

Hubbard, David A., and Glenn B. Barker, eds. *Word Biblical Commentary*. Waco, Tex.: Word Books, 1983–1988.

Kelly, Balmer H., ed. *The Layman's Bible Commentary*. 25 vols. Atlanta: John Knox Press, 1959–1960.

Laymon, Charles M. *The One Volume Commentary on the Bible*. Nashville: Abingdon Press, 1971.

Mays, James L., ed. *Harper's Bible Commentary*. San Francisco: Harper & Row, 1988.

Mays, James L., Patrick D. Miller, and Paul J. Achtemeier, eds. *Interpretation: A Bible Commentary for Teaching and Preaching*. Louisville, Ky.: Westminster/John Knox Press, 1983–1995.

Mays, James L., Carol A. Newsom, and David L. Petersen, eds. *The Old Testament Library*. Louisville, Ky.: Westminster/John Knox Press, 1961–1965.

Newsom, Carol A., and Sharon H. Ringe, eds. *The Women's Bible Commentary*. Louisville, Ky.: Westminster/John Knox Press, 1992.

Stonehouse, Ned B., ed. *The New International Commentary of the New Testament*. Grand Rapids: Wm. B. Eerdmans Publishing Co., 1955–1988.

IV.   Bible Introductions

General

Harris, Stephen, L. *Understanding the Bible*. 3d ed. Mountain View, Calif.: Mayfield Publishing Co., 1992.

Hauer, Christian E., and William A. Young. *An Introduction to the Bible: A Journey into Three Worlds*. 3d ed. Englewood Cliffs, N.J.: Prentice-Hall, 1994.

Hayes, John H. *An Introduction to the Bible*. Philadelphia: Westminster Press, 1971.

Old Testament

Anderson, Bernard. *Understanding the Old Testament*. Englewood Cliffs, N.J.: Prentice-Hall, 1966.

Drane, John. *Introduction to the Old Testament*. San Francisco: HarperCollins, 1987.

Gordon, Dane R. *The Old Testament: A Beginning Survey*. Englewood Cliffs, N.J.: Prentice-Hall, 1985.

Kuntz, J. Kenneth. *The People of Ancient Israel: An Introduction to the Old Testament Literature, History, and Thought*. New York: Harper & Row, 1974.

LaSor, William Sanford, David Allen Hubbard, and Frederic William Bush. *Old Testament Survey: The Message, Form, and Background of the Old Testament*. Grand Rapids: Wm. B. Eerdmans Publishing Co., 1982.

Soggin, J. Alberto. *Introduction to the Old Testament.* 3d ed. Louisville, Ky.: Westminster/John Knox Press, 1989.

New Testament

Carmody, John, Denise Lardner Carmody, and Gregory A. Robbins. *Exploring the New Testament.* Englewood Cliffs, N.J.: Prentice-Hall, 1986.

Guthrie, Donald. *New Testament Introduction.* Revised. Downers Grove, Ill.: InterVarsity Press, 1990.

Harris, Steven L. *The New Testament: A Student's Introduction.* Mountain View, Calif.: Mayfield Publishing Co., 1988.

Kee, Howard Clark. *Understanding the New Testament.* Englewood Cliffs, N.J.: Prentice-Hall, 1983.

Koester, Helmut. *Introduction to the New Testament.* 2 vols. Philadelphia: Fortress Press, 1982.

Price, James L. *The New Testament: Its Theology and History.* New York: Macmillan Publishing Co., 1987.

V.   Bible Atlases

May, Herbert G. *Oxford Bible Atlas.* 2d ed. New York: Oxford University Press, 1974.

Pritchard, James B., ed. *The Harper Atlas of the Bible.* New York: Harper & Row, 1987.

Van der Woude, A. S., ed. *The World of the Bible.* Grand Rapids: Wm. B. Eerdmans Publishing Co., 1986.

Wright, George Ernest, and Floyd V. Filson. *The Westminster Historical Handbook and Atlas to the Bible.* Philadelphia: Westminster Press, 1956.

VI. Bible Study Guides

Alexander, David, and Pat Alexander. *Eerdmans Handbook to the Bible.* Grand Rapids: Wm. B. Eerdmans Publishing Co., 1983.

Beck, Madeline H., and Lamar Williamson, Jr. *Mastering New Testament Facts.* 4 vols. Atlanta: John Knox Press, 1973.

Marshall, Celia Brewer. *A Guide through the Old Testament.* Louisville, Ky.: Westminster/John Knox Press, 1989.

———. *A Guide through the New Testament.* Louisville, Ky.: Westminster/John Knox Press, 1964.

Piet, John H. *A Path through the Bible.* Philadelphia: Westminster Press, 1981.

Taylor, Mark D. *The Complete Book of Bible Literacy.* Wheaton, Ill.: Tyndale Publishers, 1992.

Weber, Hans-Ruedi. *Experiments with Bible Study.* Philadelphia: Westminster Press, 1981.

VII.   Biblical Theology

Old Testament

Eichrodt, Walter. *Theology of the Old Testament.* 2 vols. Philadelphia: Westminster Press, 1961.

Hayes, John H., and Frederick C. Prussner. *Old Testament Theology: Its History and Development.* Atlanta: John Knox Press, 1985.

von Rad, Gerhard. *Old Testament Theology.* 2 vols. New York: Harper & Row, 1962.

New Testament

Goppelt, Leonhard. *Theology of the New Testament.* 2 vols. Grand Rapids: Wm. B. Eerdmans Publishing Co., 1981.

Jeremias, Joachim. *New Testament Theology: The Proclamation of Jesus.* New York: Charles Scribner's Sons, 1971.

Kittel, Gerhard, ed. *Theological Dictionary of the New Testament.* 9 vols. Grand Rapids: Wm. B. Eerdmans Publishing Co., 1964–1974.

Kittel, Gerhard, and Gerhard Friedrich, eds. *Theological Dictionary of the New Testament.* Grand Rapids: Wm. B. Eerdmans Publishing Co., 1985.

VIII.   Bible Concordances

Kohlenberger, John R. *The NRSV Concordance.* Grand Rapids: Zondervan Publishing House, 1991.

Metzger, Bruce M. *NRSV Exhaustive Concordance.* Nashville: Thomas Nelson Publishers, 1991.

Strong, James. *The New Strong's Exhaustive Concordance of the Bible.* Nashville: Thomas Nelson Publishers, 1990.

Young, Robert. *Young's Analytical Concordance to the Bible.* Grand Rapids: Wm. B. Eerdmans Publishing Co., 1970.

Whitaker, Richard E., compiler. *The Eerdmans Analytical Concordance of the Bible: To the Revised Standard Version.* Grand Rapids: Wm. B. Eerdmans Publishing Co., 1988.

Notes

Chapter 1

1. See E. D. Hirsch, *Cultural Literacy: What Every American Needs to Know* (Boston: Houghton Mifflin Co., 1987).

2. See James Walther, *KERYGMA: Bible Study in Depth* (Toronto: United Church of Canada, 1977). For information about the KERYGMA program, write 300 Mt. Lebanon Blvd., Suite 205, Pittsburgh, PA 15234.

Chapter 2

1. See Robert Alter and Frank Kermode, eds., *The Literary Guide to the Bible* (Cambridge, Mass.: Belknap Press of Harvard University Press, 1987).

2. We use B.C.E. (Before the Common Era) and C.E. (Common Era) throughout this volume.

3. Christian E. Hauer and William A. Young, *An Introduction to the Bible: A Journey into Three Worlds,* 3d ed. (Englewood Cliffs, N.J.: Prentice-Hall, 1994), 3.

4. See, for example, Daniel P. Fuller, *The Unity of the Bible* (Grand Rapids: Zondervan Publishing House, 1992), and H. H. Rowley, *The Unity of the Bible* (Philadelphia: Westminster Press, 1953).

5. Duncan S. Ferguson, *Biblical Hermeneutics: An Introduction* (Atlanta: John Knox Press, 1986), 23–26.

6. See Paul D. Hanson, *The Diversity of Scripture: A Theological Interpretation* (Philadelphia: Fortress Press, 1982).

7. Ferguson, *Biblical Hermeneutics,* 26–28.

8. Ibid., 28–30.

9. Ibid., 30–39.

10. See Henning Graf Reventlow, *The Authority of the Bible and the Rise of the Modern World* (Philadelphia: Fortress Press, 1985).

11. See Jack B. Rogers and Donald K. McKim, *The Authority and Interpretation of the Bible: An Historical Approach* (San Francisco: Harper & Row, 1979), and Robert M. Grant, *A Short History of the Interpretation of the Bible,* 2d ed. (Philadelphia: Fortress Press, 1984).

12. See Hauer and Young, *Introduction to the Bible,* 32–53.

13. Ibid., 34.

Chapter 3

1. Paul J. Achtemeier, ed., *Harper's Bible Dictionary* (San Francisco: Harper & Row, 1985), 983–86.

Chapter 4

1. Stephen L. Harris, *Understanding the Bible* (Mountain View, Calif.: Mayfield Publishing Co., 1992), 93–94.

Chapter 6

1. Interest in "uncovering" the historical Jesus recurs from time to time. The original "quest" was largely a late nineteenth-century movement, one that was fundamentally flawed. At mid-twentieth century, a "new quest" attempted to avoid the pitfalls of the earlier movement. Currently, there is another quest, one driven largely by the attempt to place Jesus in his first-century Jewish context.

2. Harris, *Understanding the Bible*, 270–72.